Real World
Colouring Book
For Advanced Users & Adults

50 Images

**Created From Real Life Photos
For You To Colour As You Please.**

ISBN 978-0-359-83314-6
90000
9 780359 833146

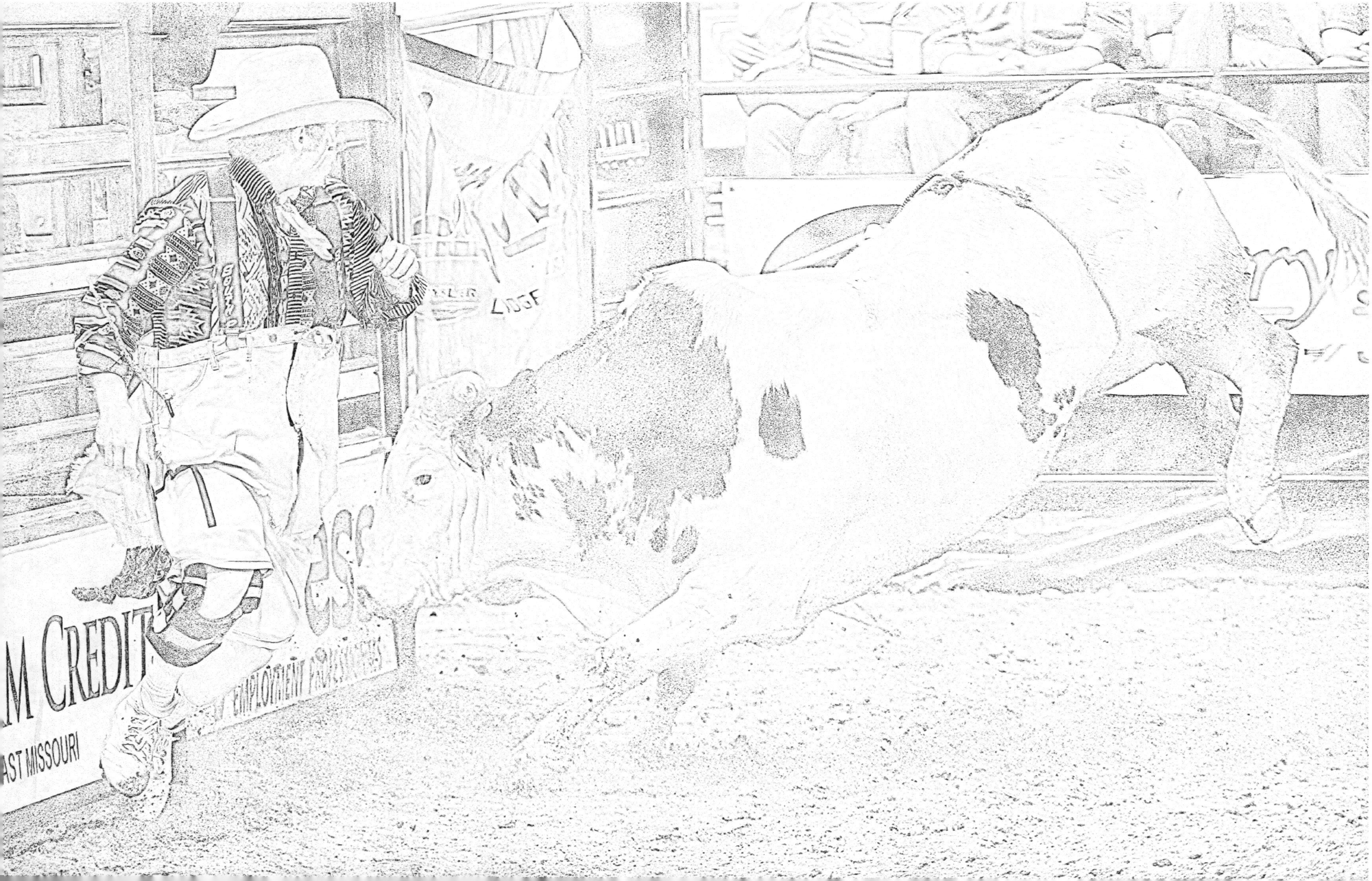
M CREDIT
AST MISSOURI

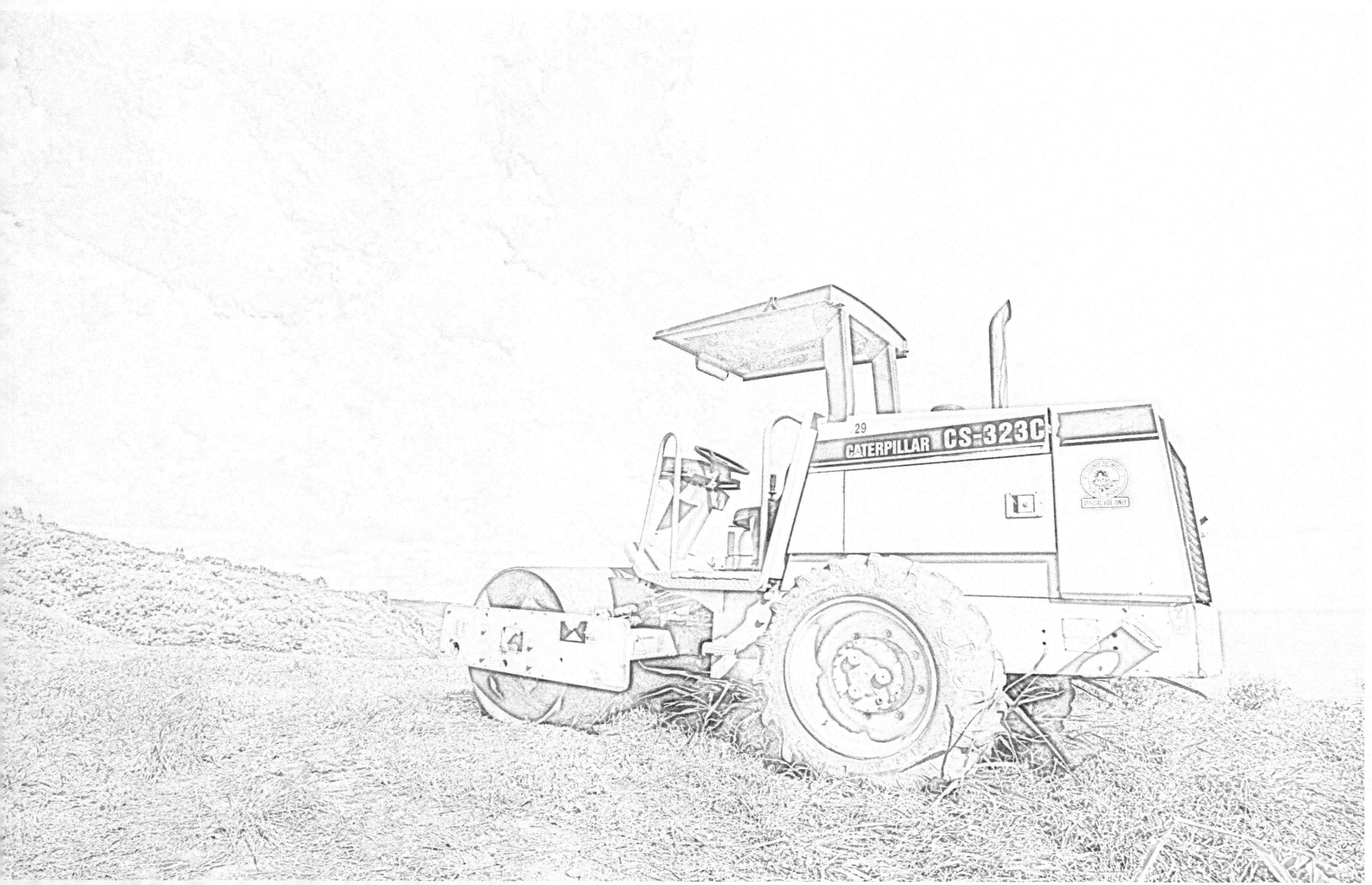

29
CATERPILLAR
CS-323C
OFFICIAL USE ONLY

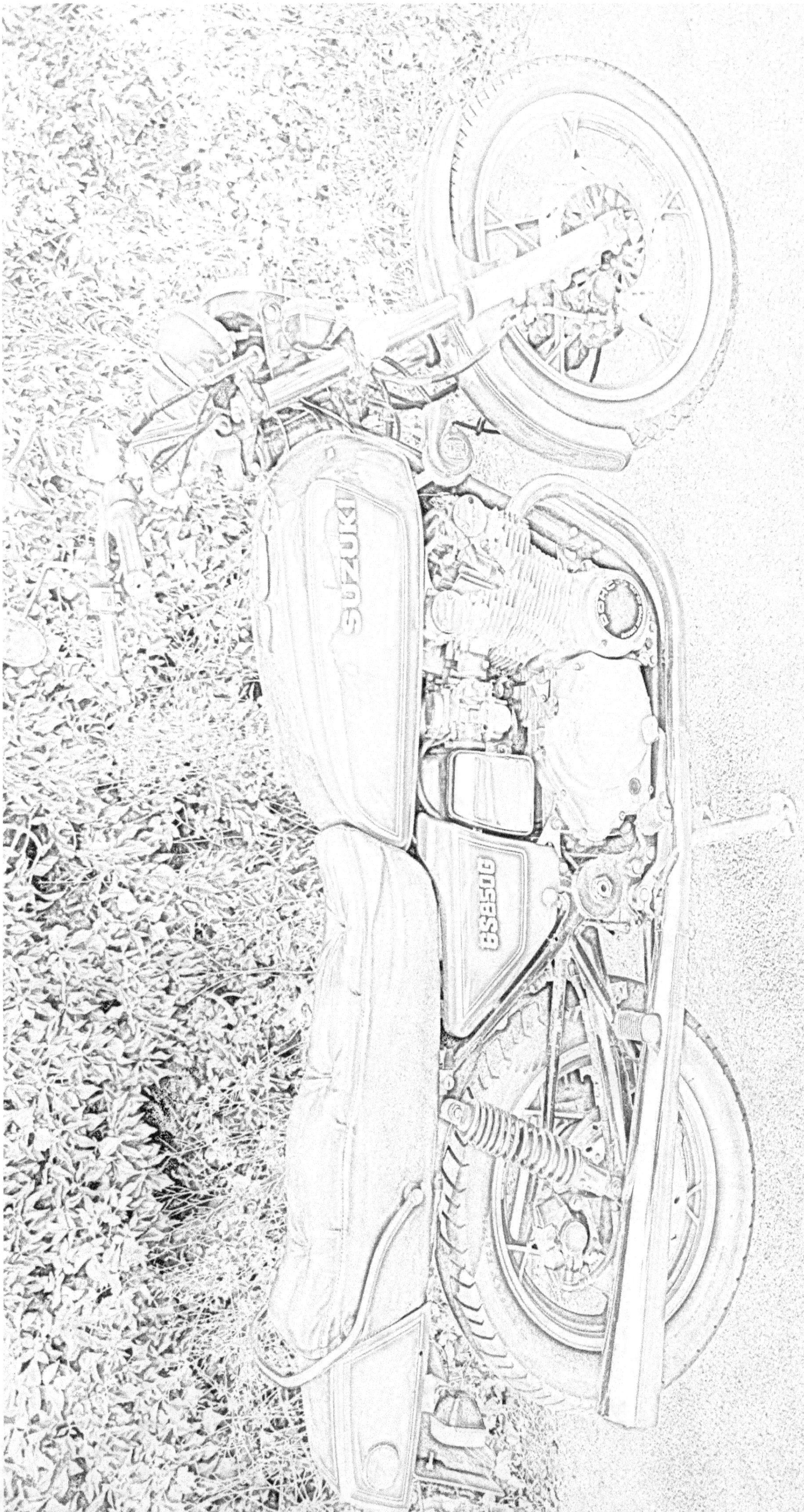
SUZUKI
GS850G

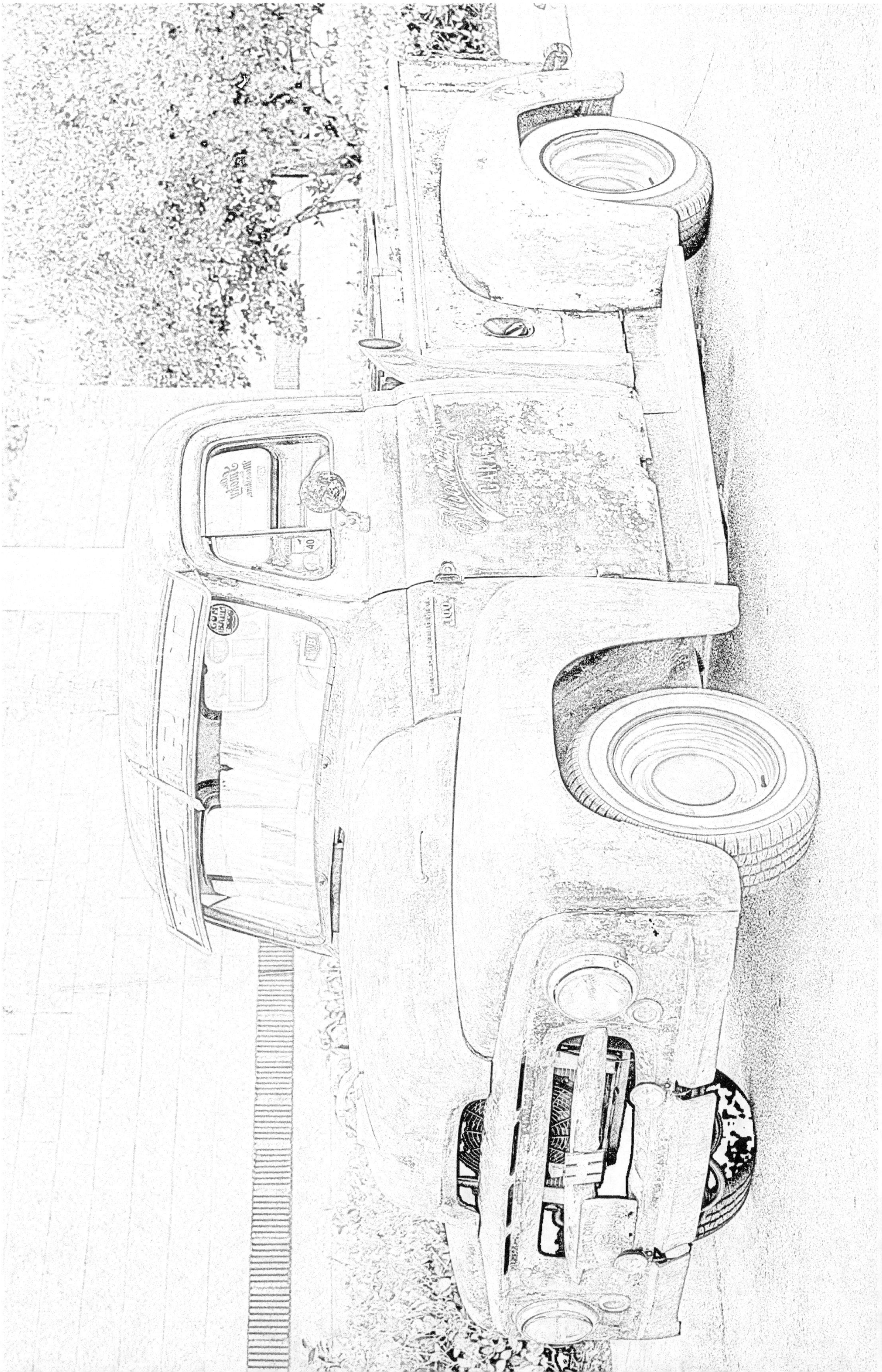

A

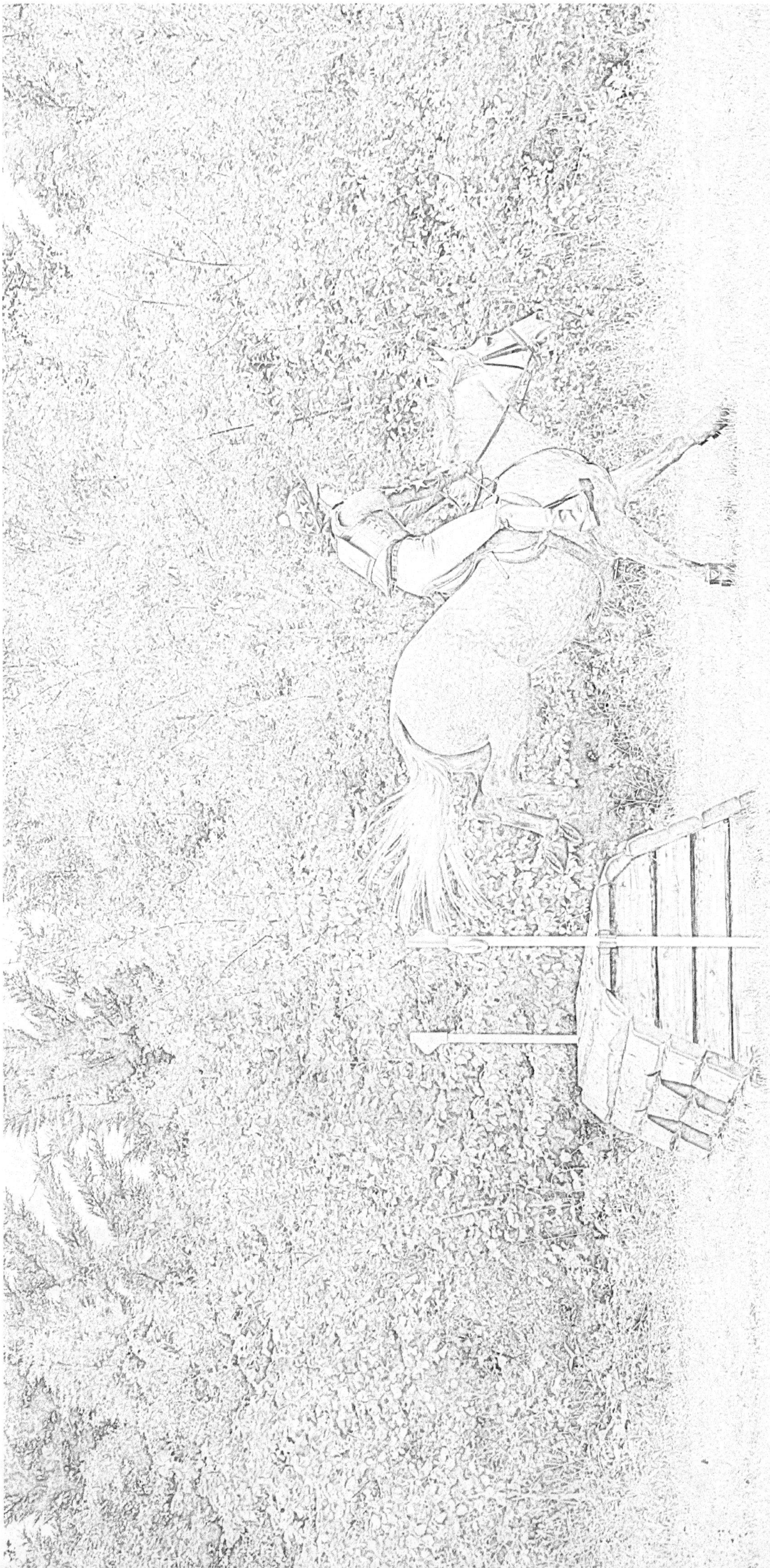

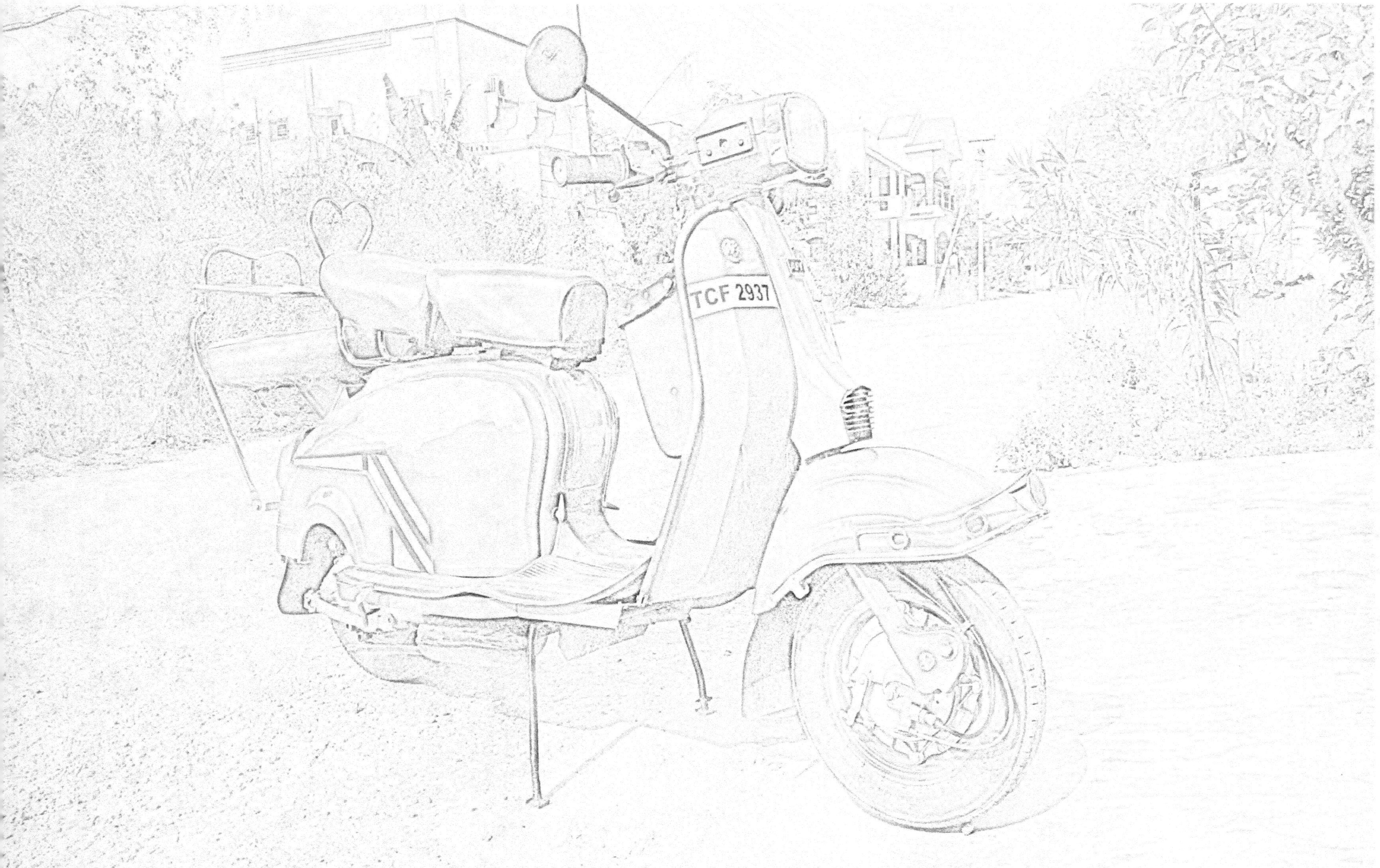
TCF 2937

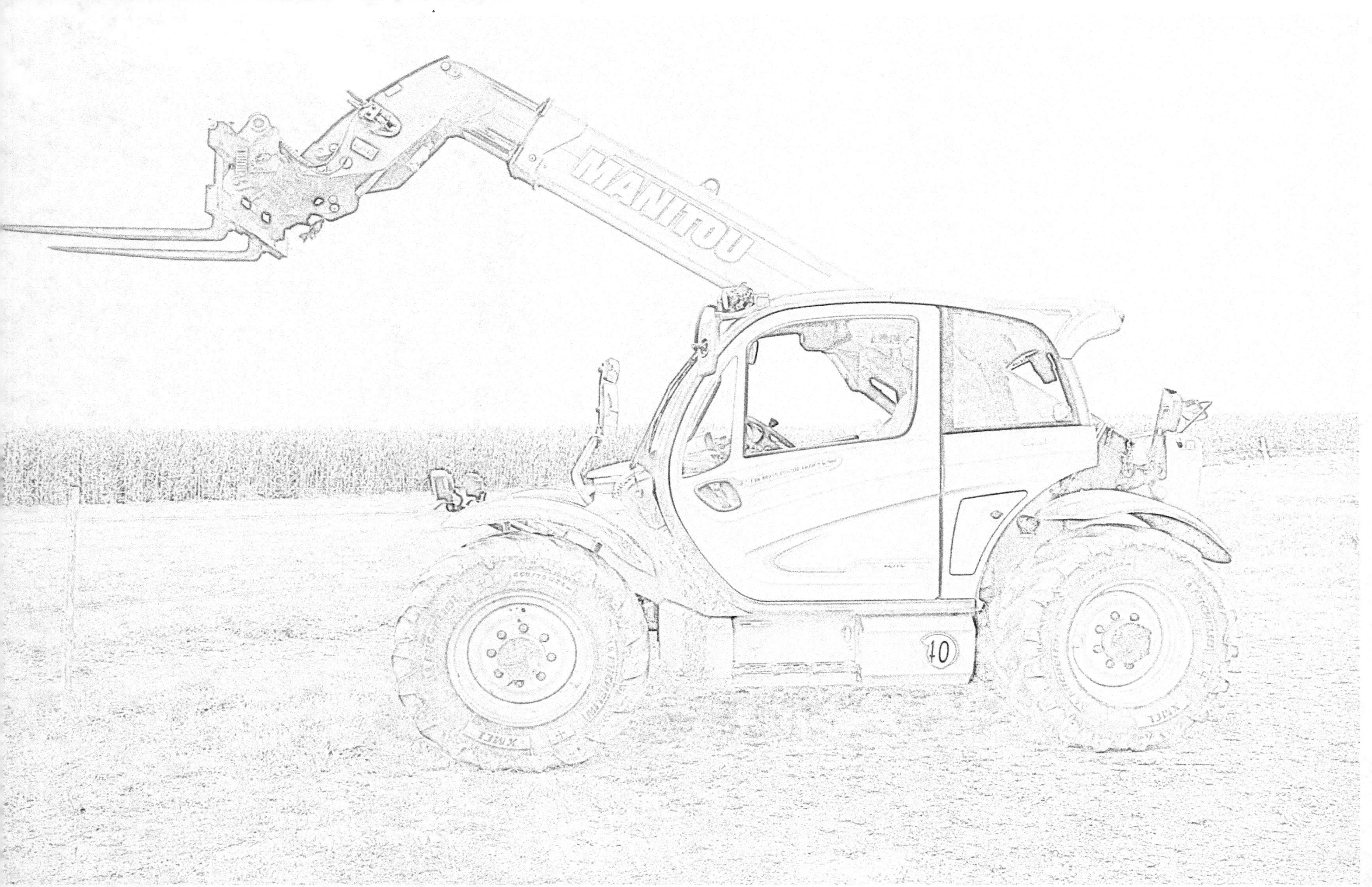
MANITOU
40

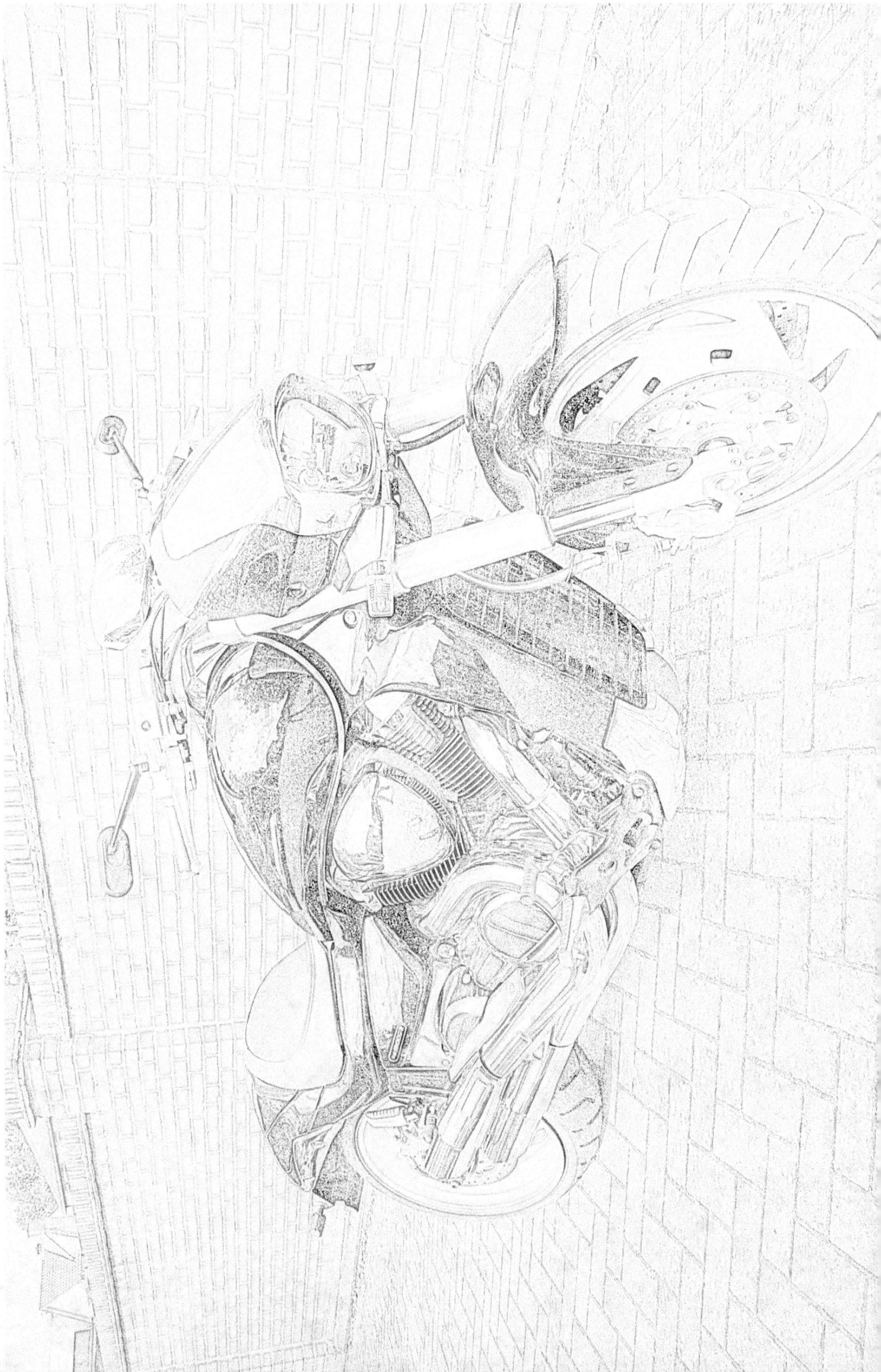

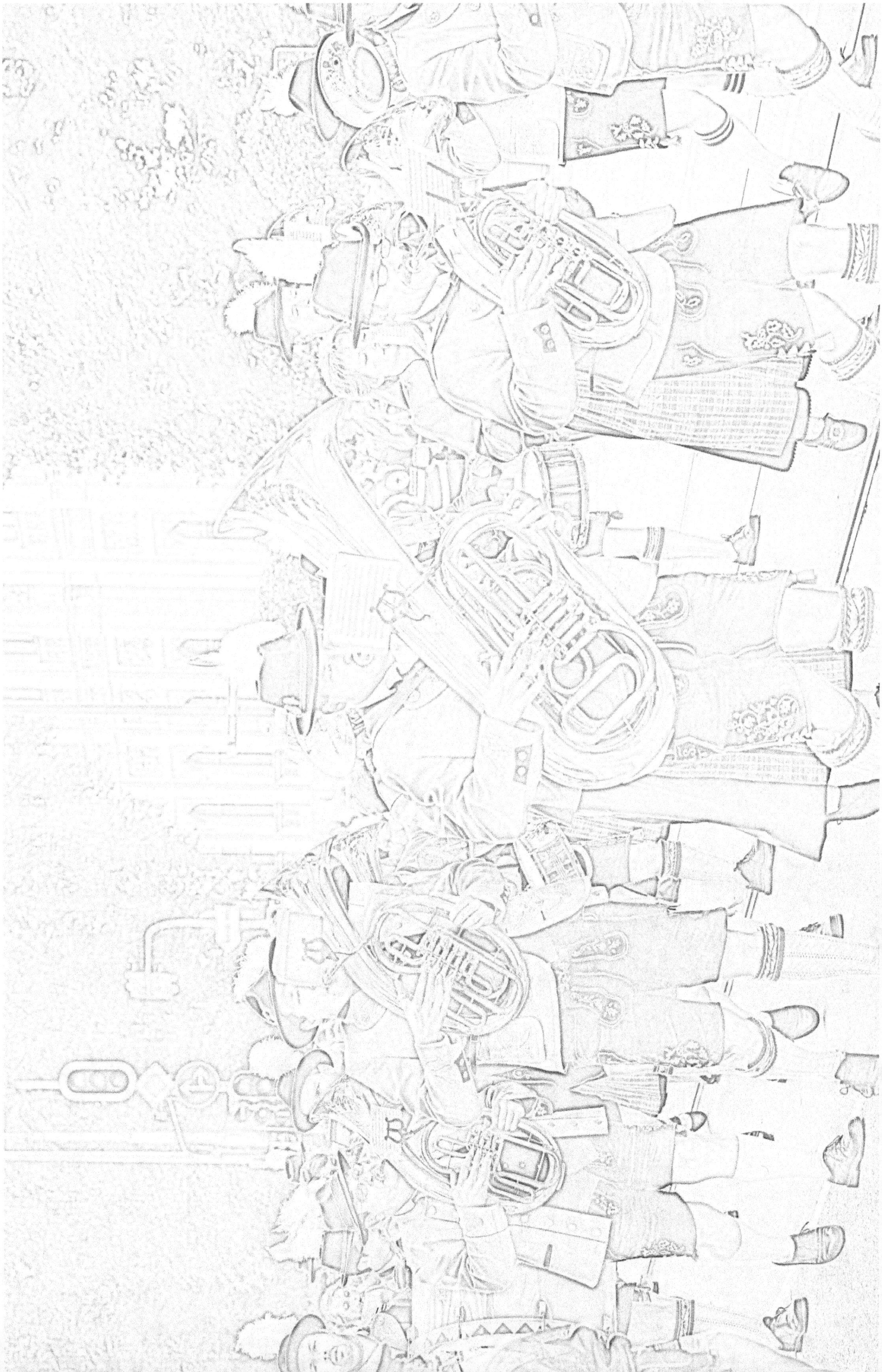

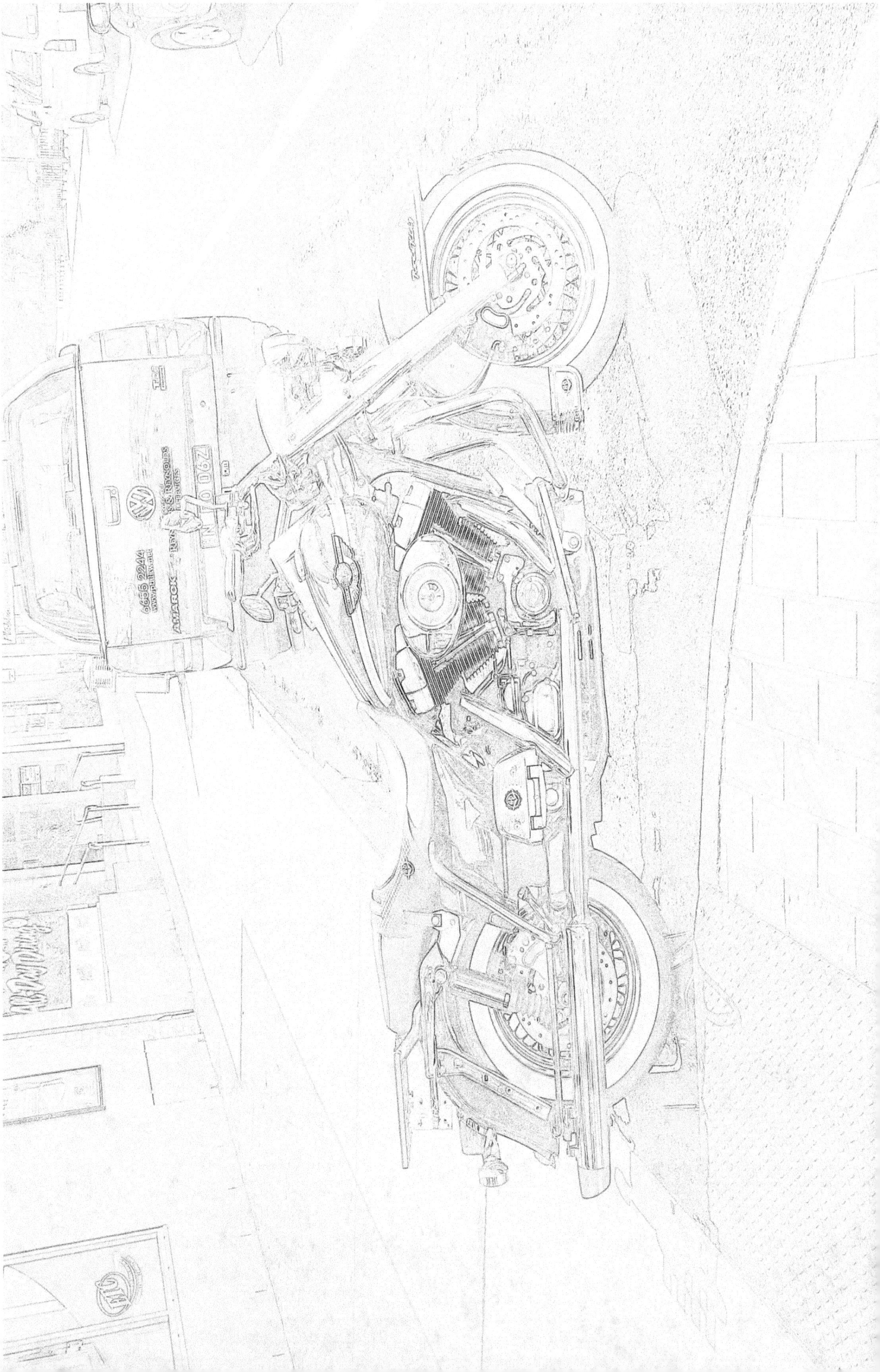
AMAROK
6656 2244

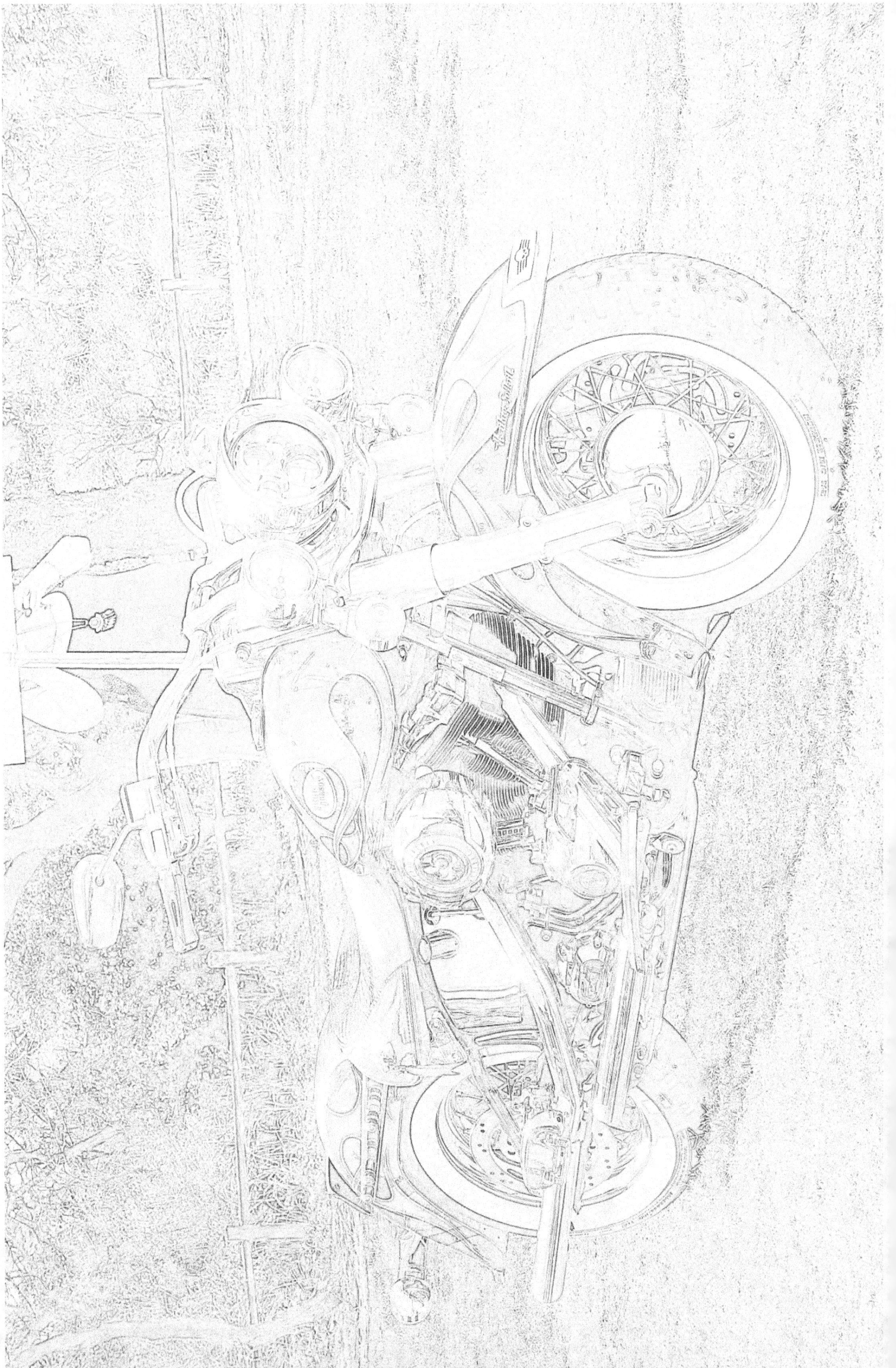

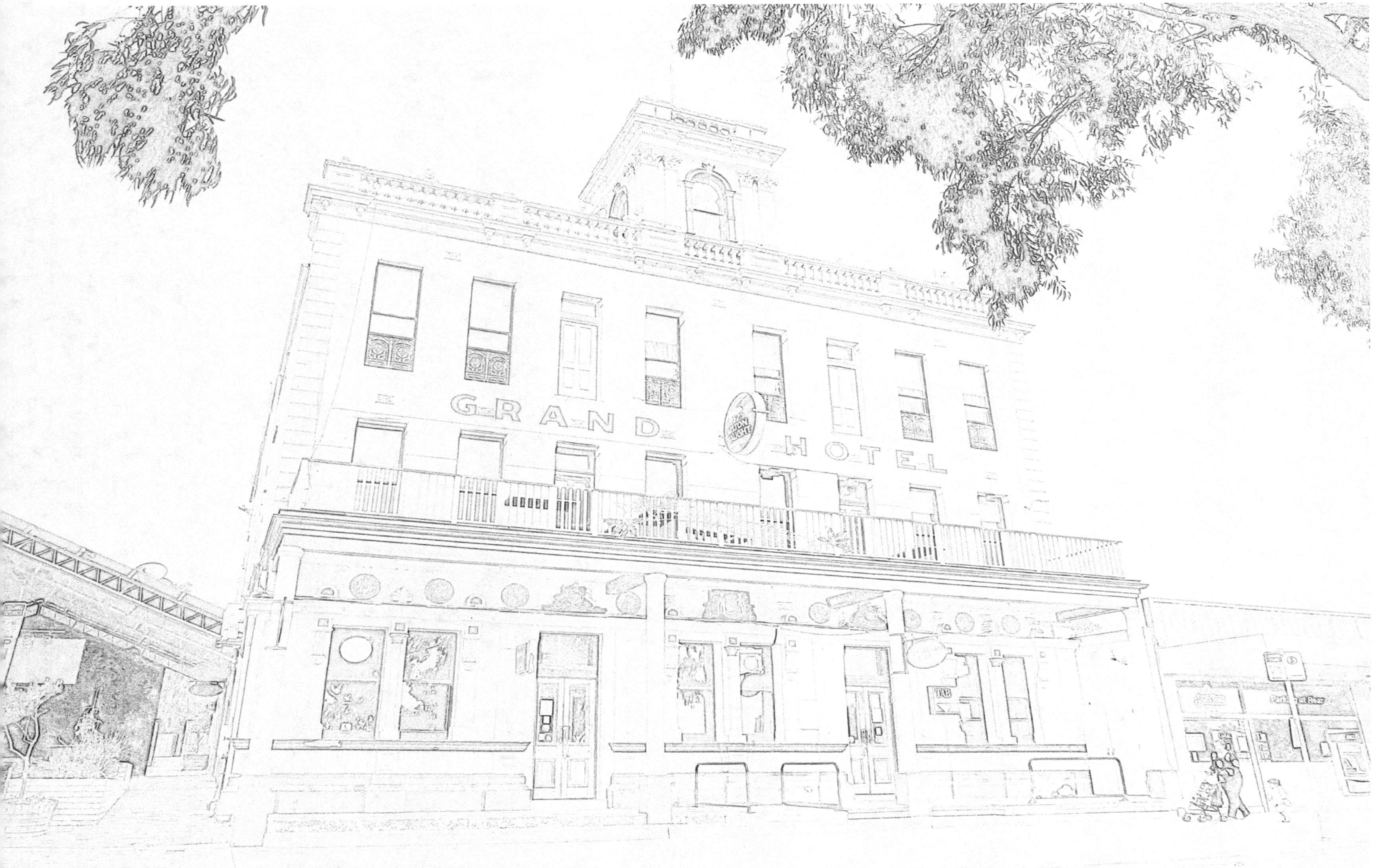
GRAND HOTEL
TAB
Parking at Rear

GALLERY
PASQUINI'S
Point Lonsdale

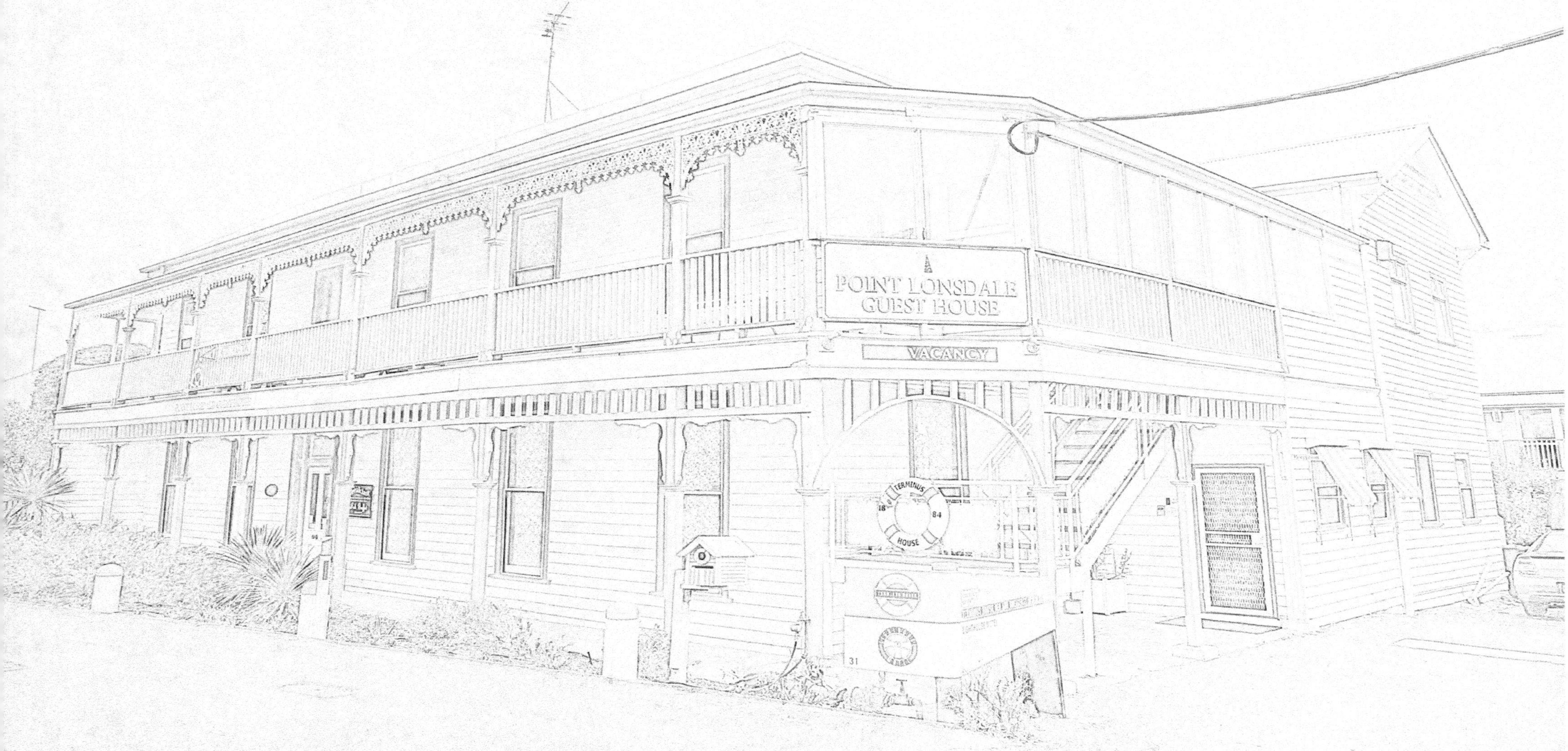
POINT LONSDALE
GUEST HOUSE
VACANCY
TERMINUS
18
84
HOUSE
31

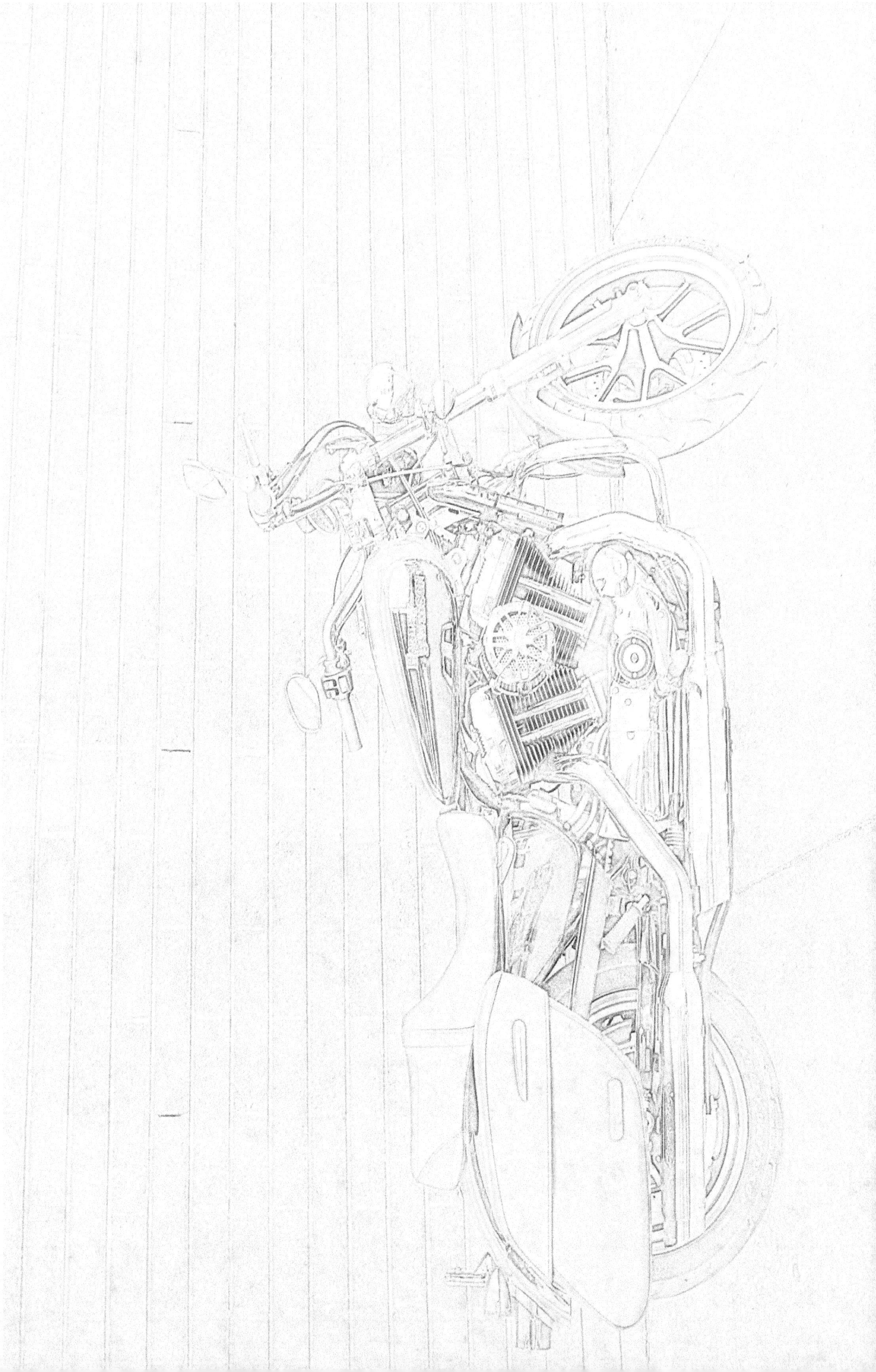

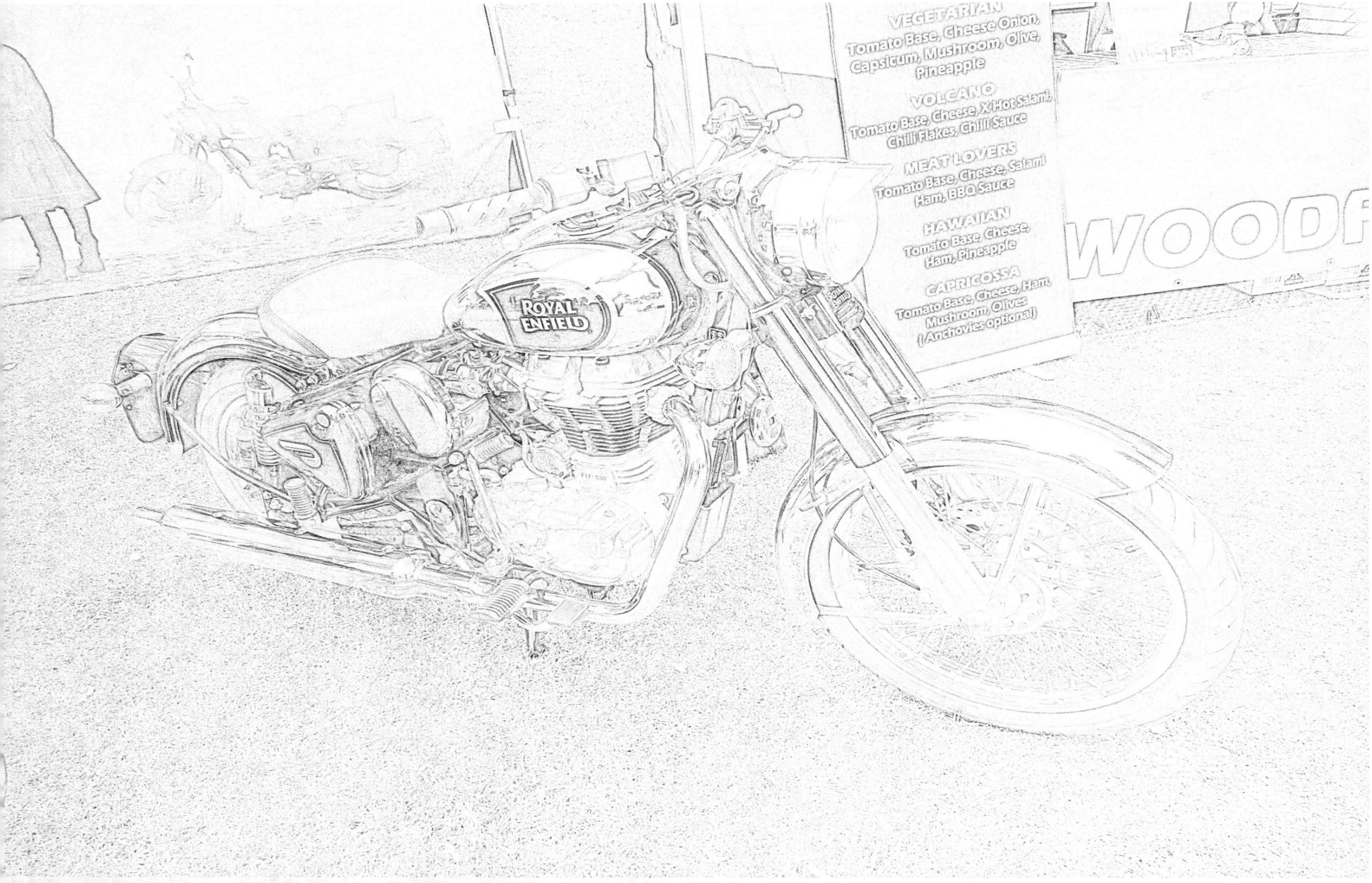
VEGETARIAN
Tomato Base, Cheese Onion, Capsicum, Mushroom, Olive, Pineapple
VOLCANO
Tomato Base, Cheese, X Hot Salami, Chilli Flakes, Chilli Sauce
MEAT LOVERS
Tomato Base, Cheese, Salami Ham, BBQ Sauce
HAWAIIAN
Tomato Base, Cheese, Ham, Pineapple
CAPRICOSSA
Tomato Base, Cheese, Ham, Mushroom, Olives
(Anchovies optional)
ROYAL ENFIELD

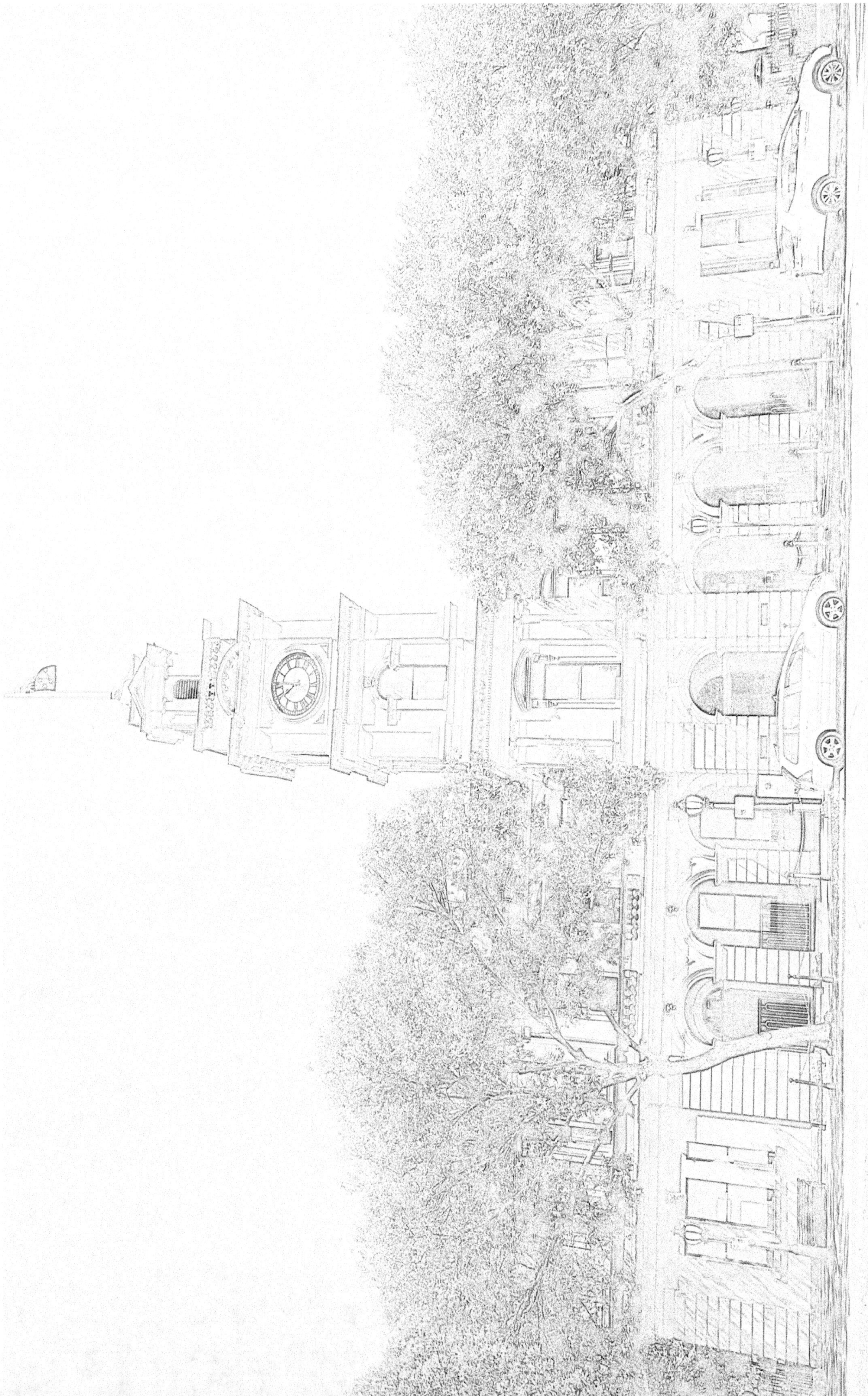

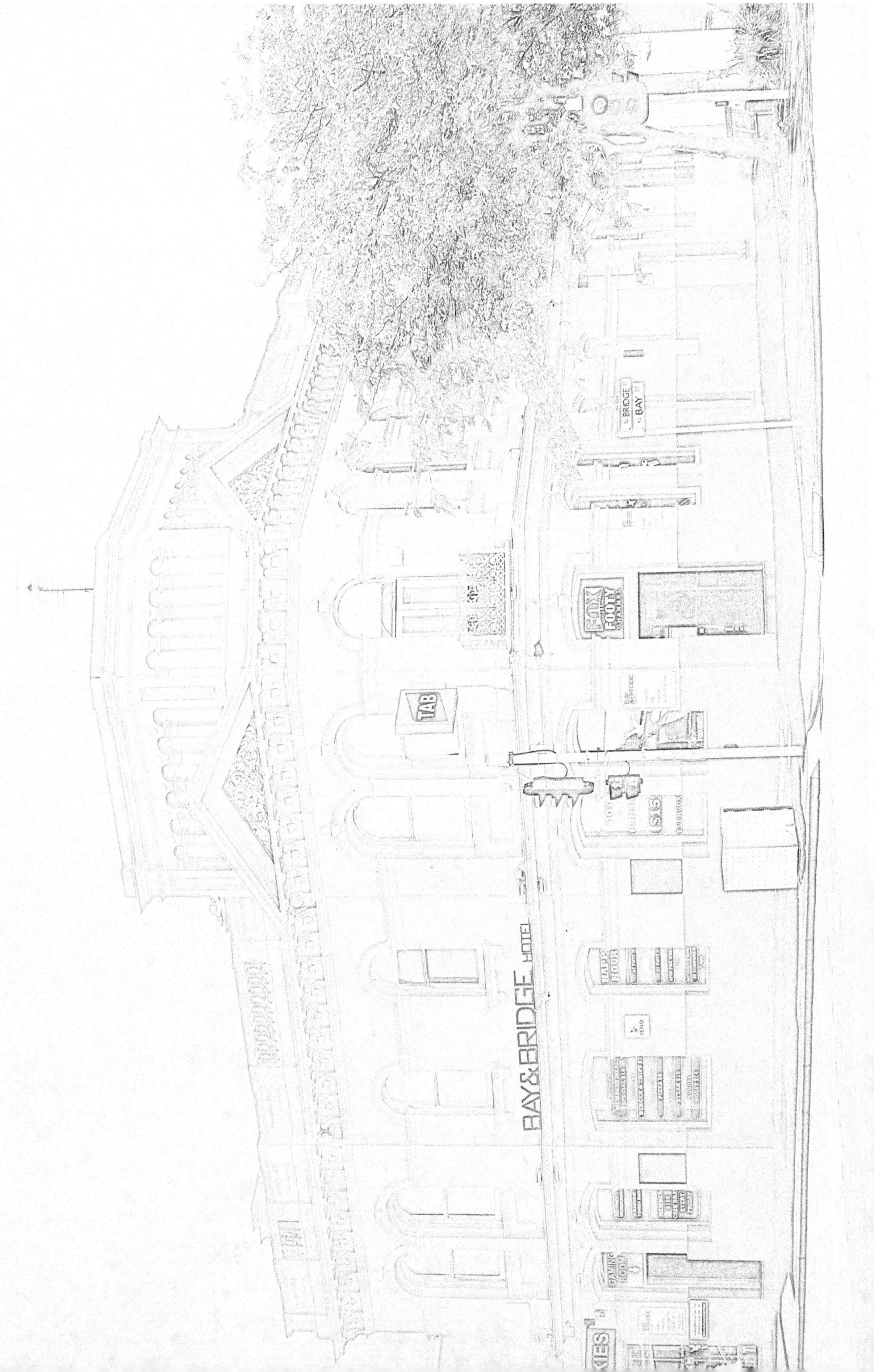
BAY&BRIDGE HOTEL
TAB
FOX FOOTY CHANNEL
BRIDGE
BAY ST
$15
HAPPY HOUR
KENO
GAMING ROOM

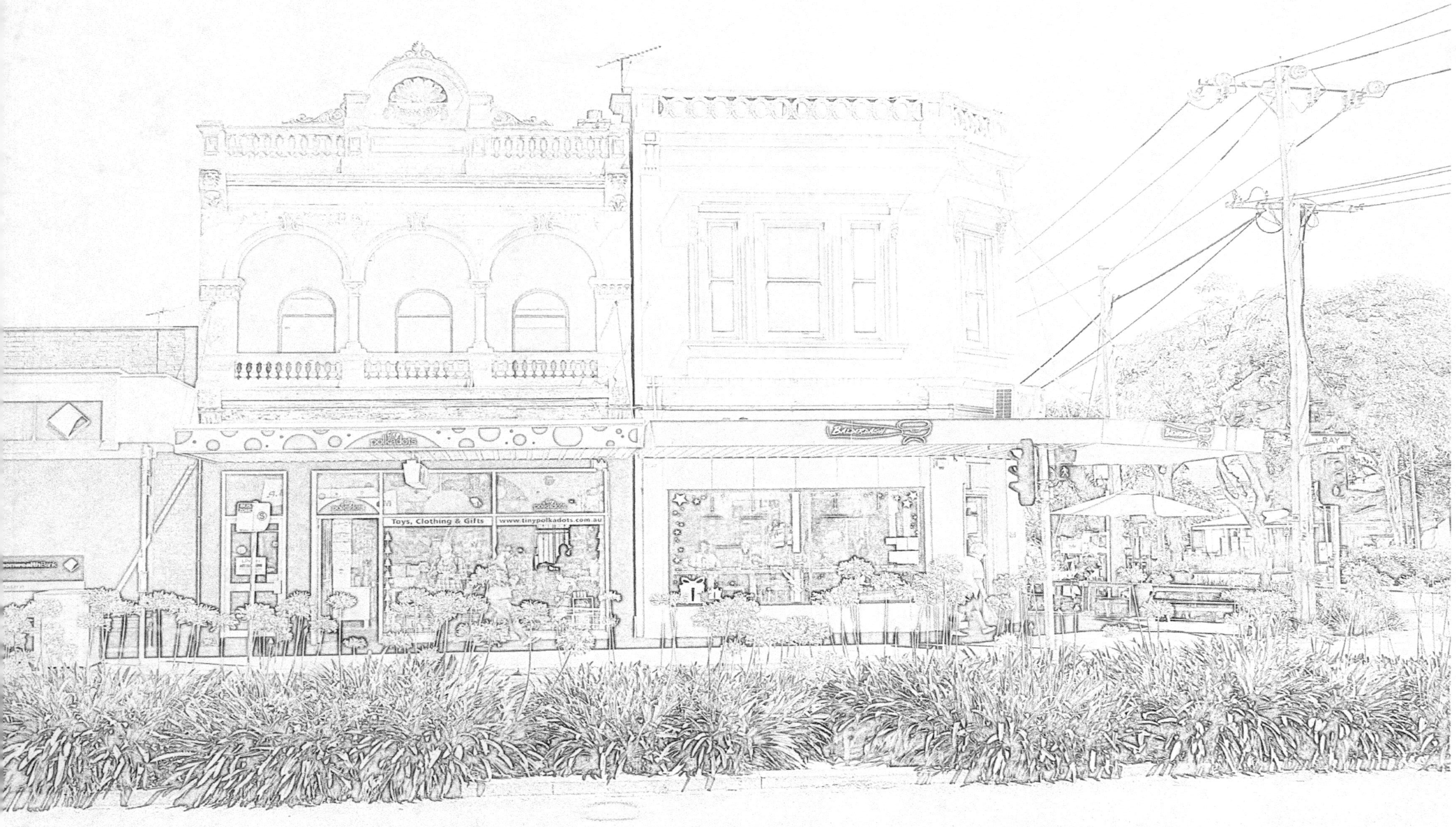

polkadots
Toys, Clothing & Gifts
www.tinypolkadots.com.au

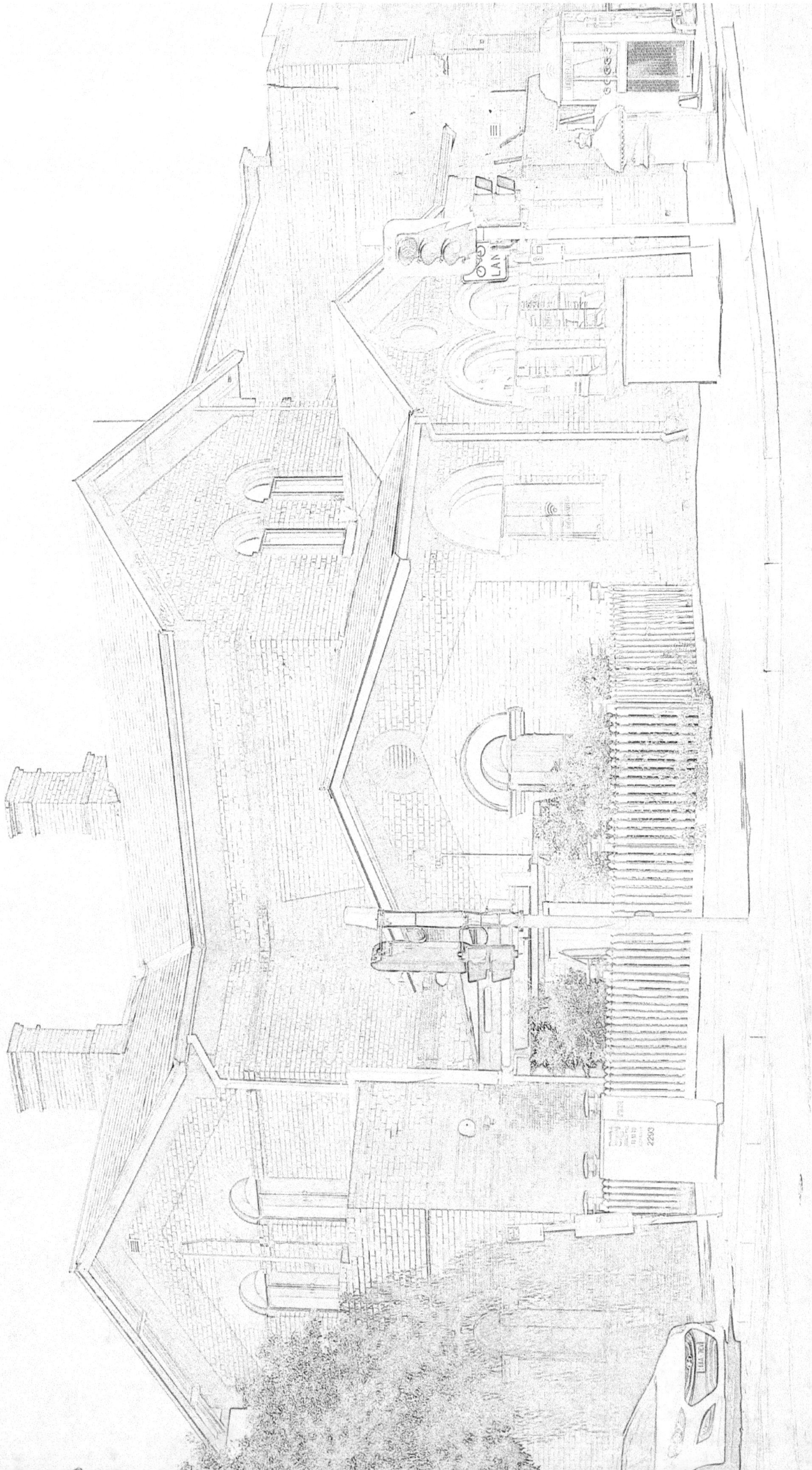
2293

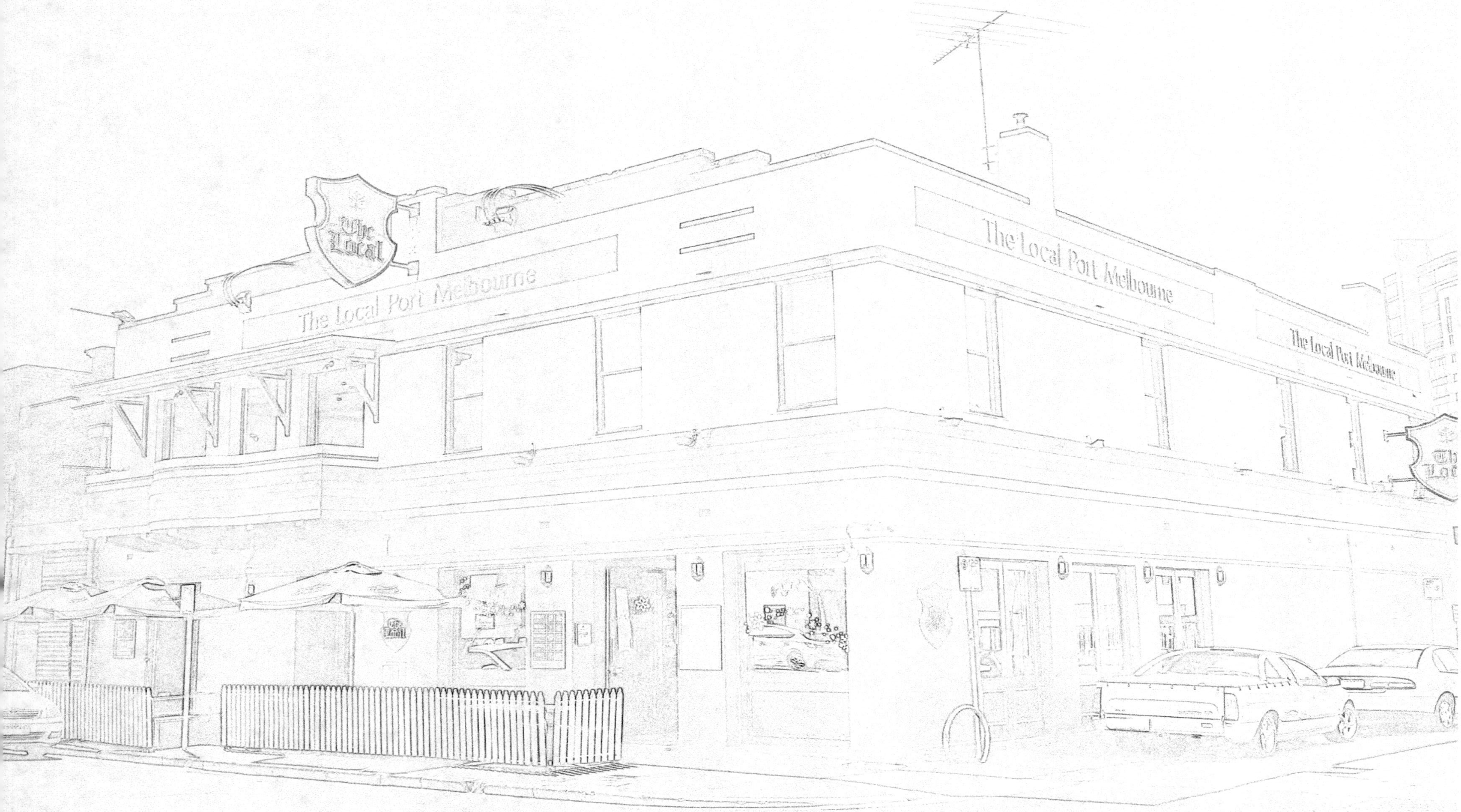
The Local
The Local Port Melbourne
The Local Port Melbourne
The Local Port Melbourne

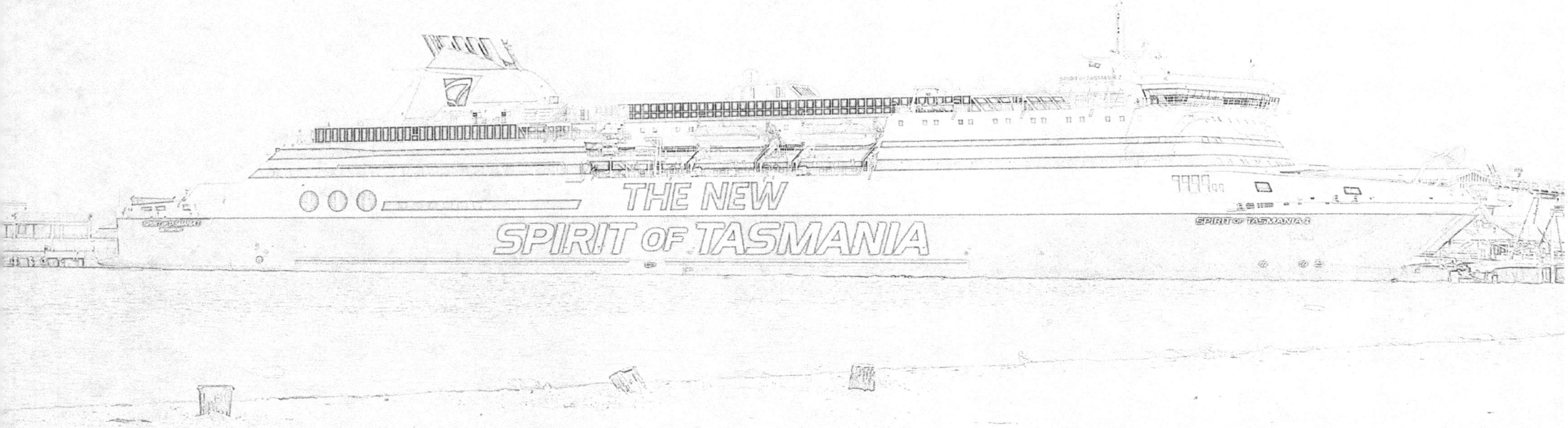
THE NEW
SPIRIT OF TASMANIA

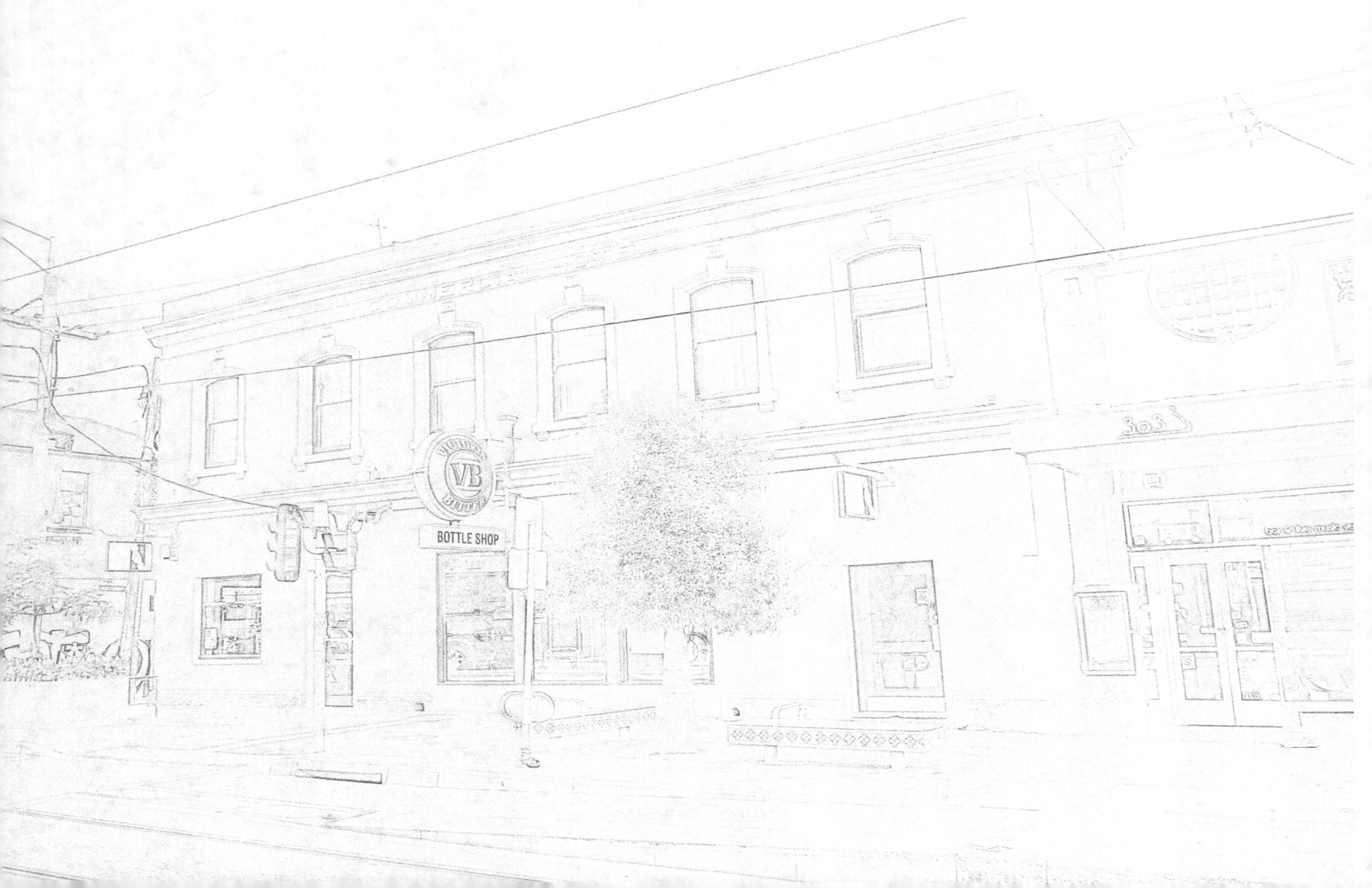
VB
BOTTLE SHOP
303

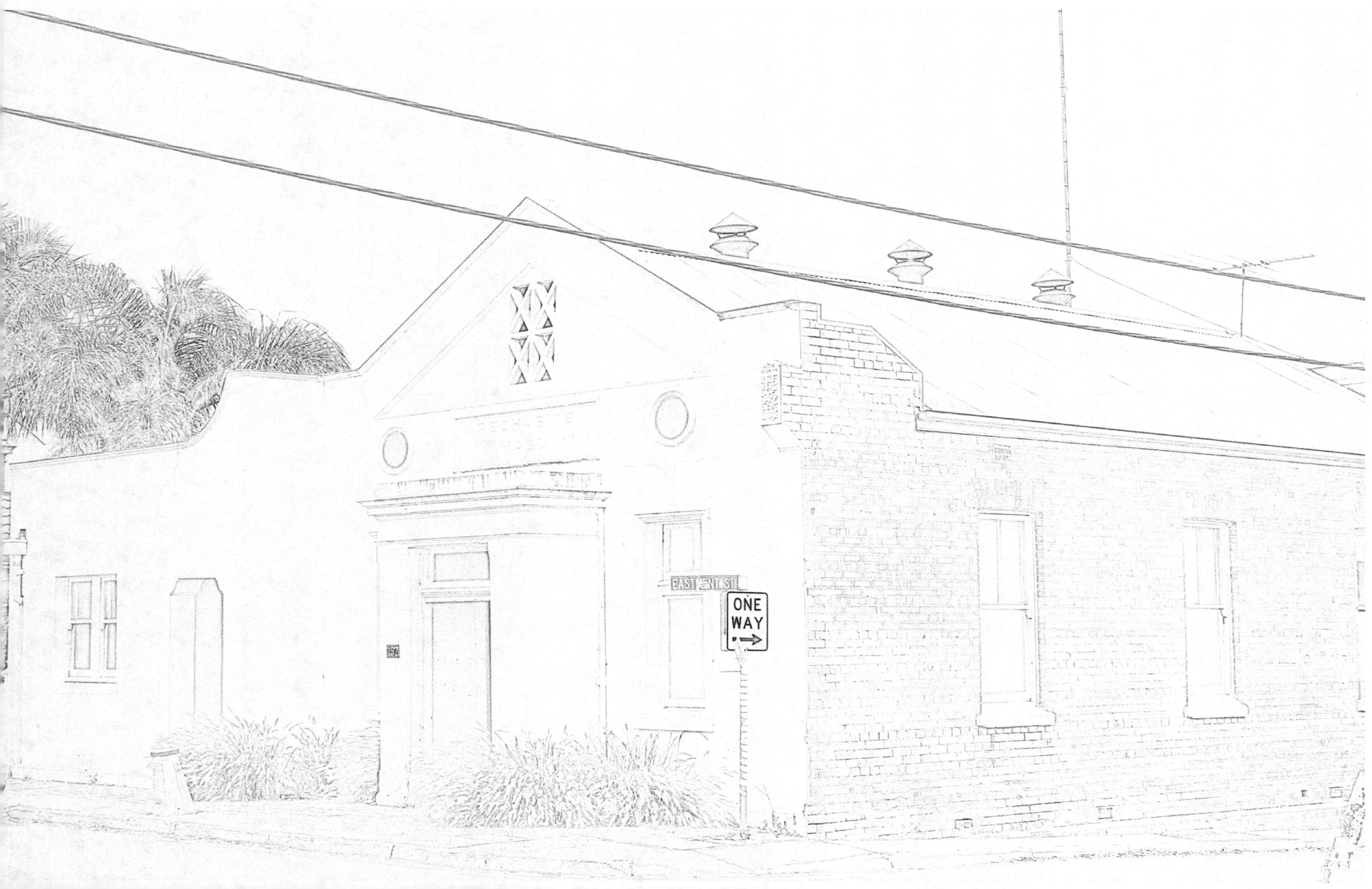
ONE
WAY

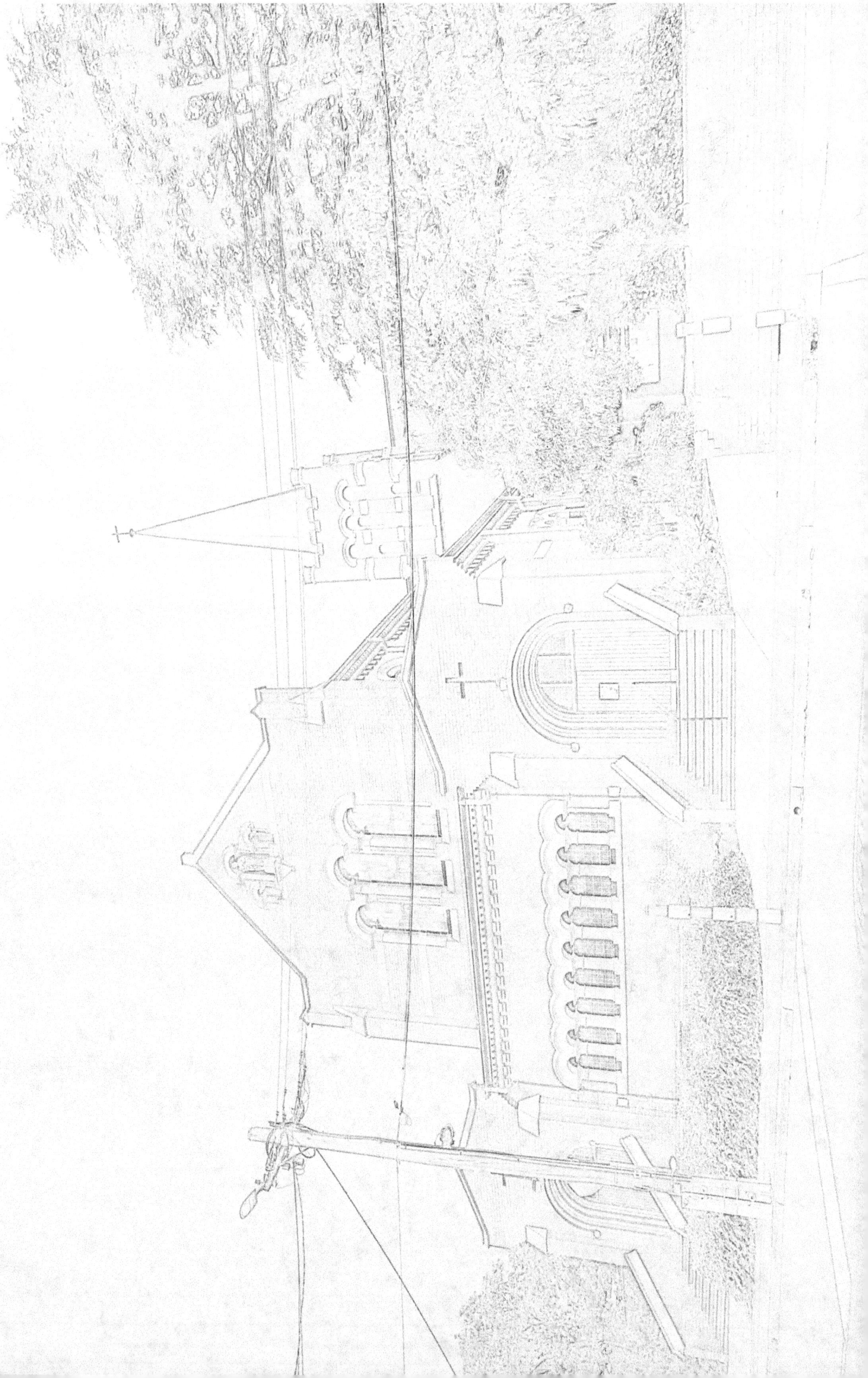

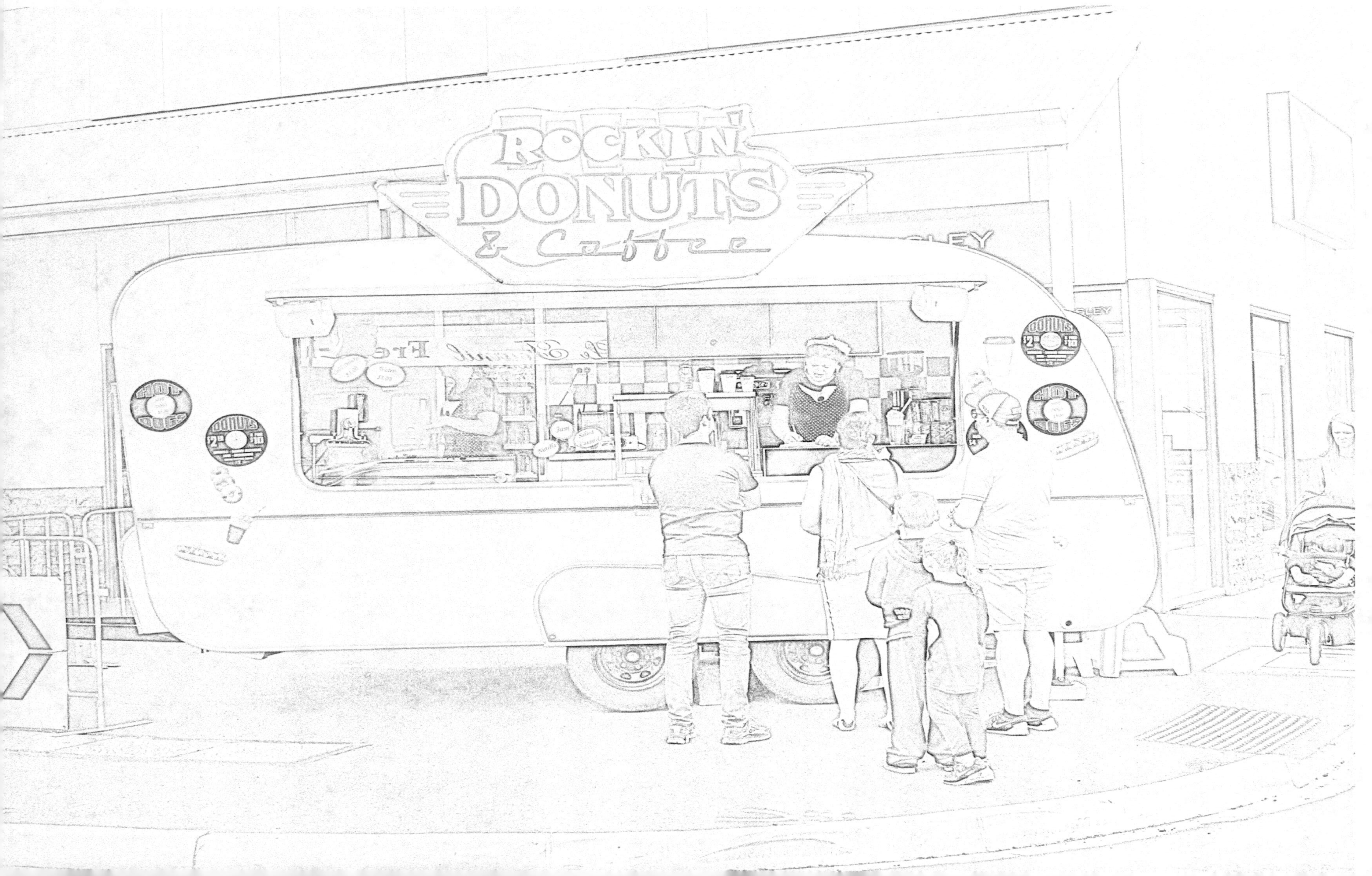

ROCKIN'
DONUTS
& Coffee
HOT DOGS
DONUTS

DEAKIN
Worldly
Ford
BRIGHTON FORD
deakin.edu.au

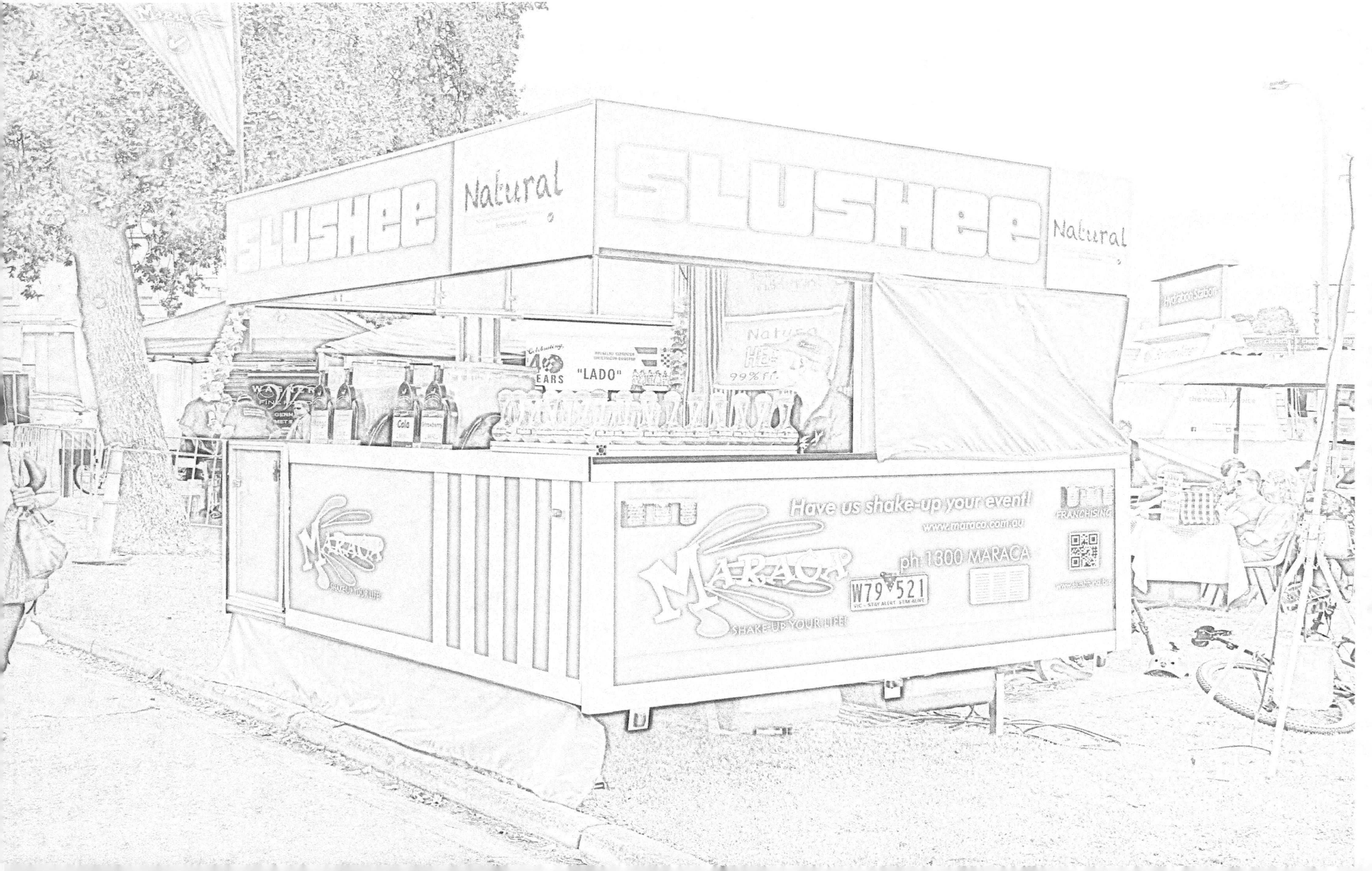
SLUSHEE
Natural
SLUSHEE
Natural
"LADO"
Cola
Have us shake-up your event!
www.maraca.com.au
ph 1800 MARACA
FRANCHISING
MARACA
SHAKE-UP YOUR LIFE!
W79 521
VIC - STAY ALERT STAY ALIVE
MARACA
SHAKE-UP YOUR LIFE!

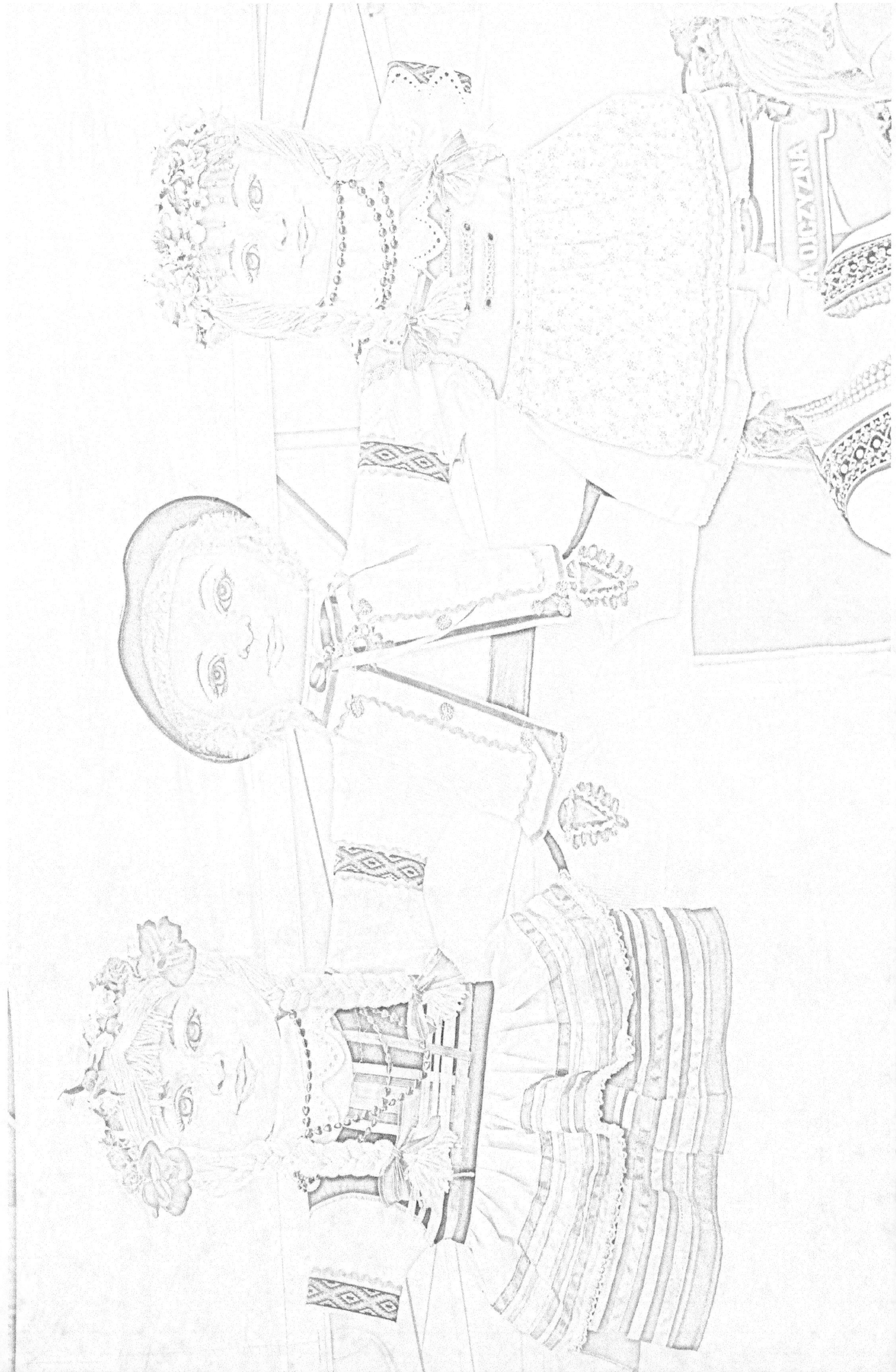
OJCZYZNA

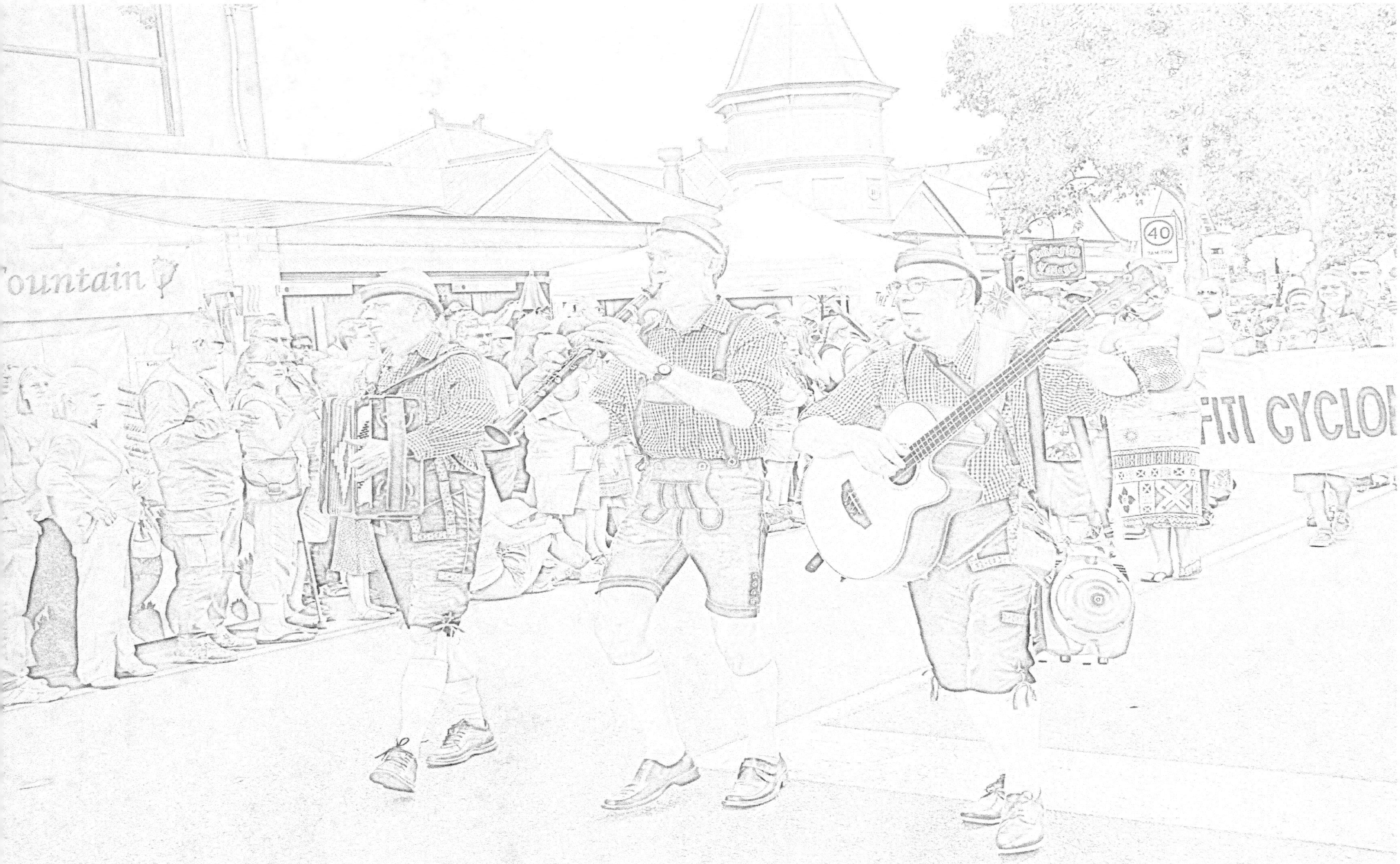
Fountain
40
FIJI CYCLO

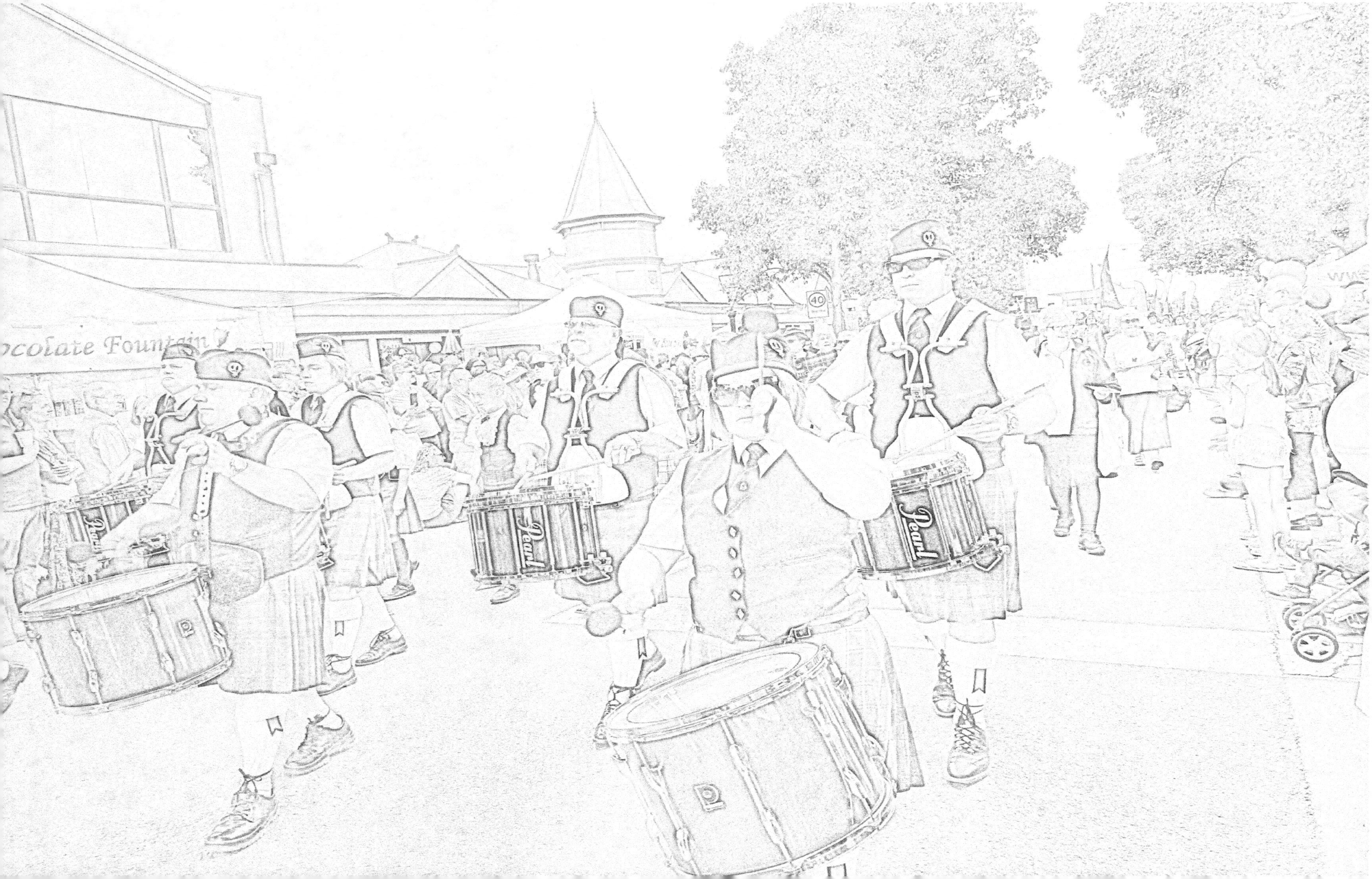
ocolate Fountain
40
Pearl
Pearl
Pearl
Pearl

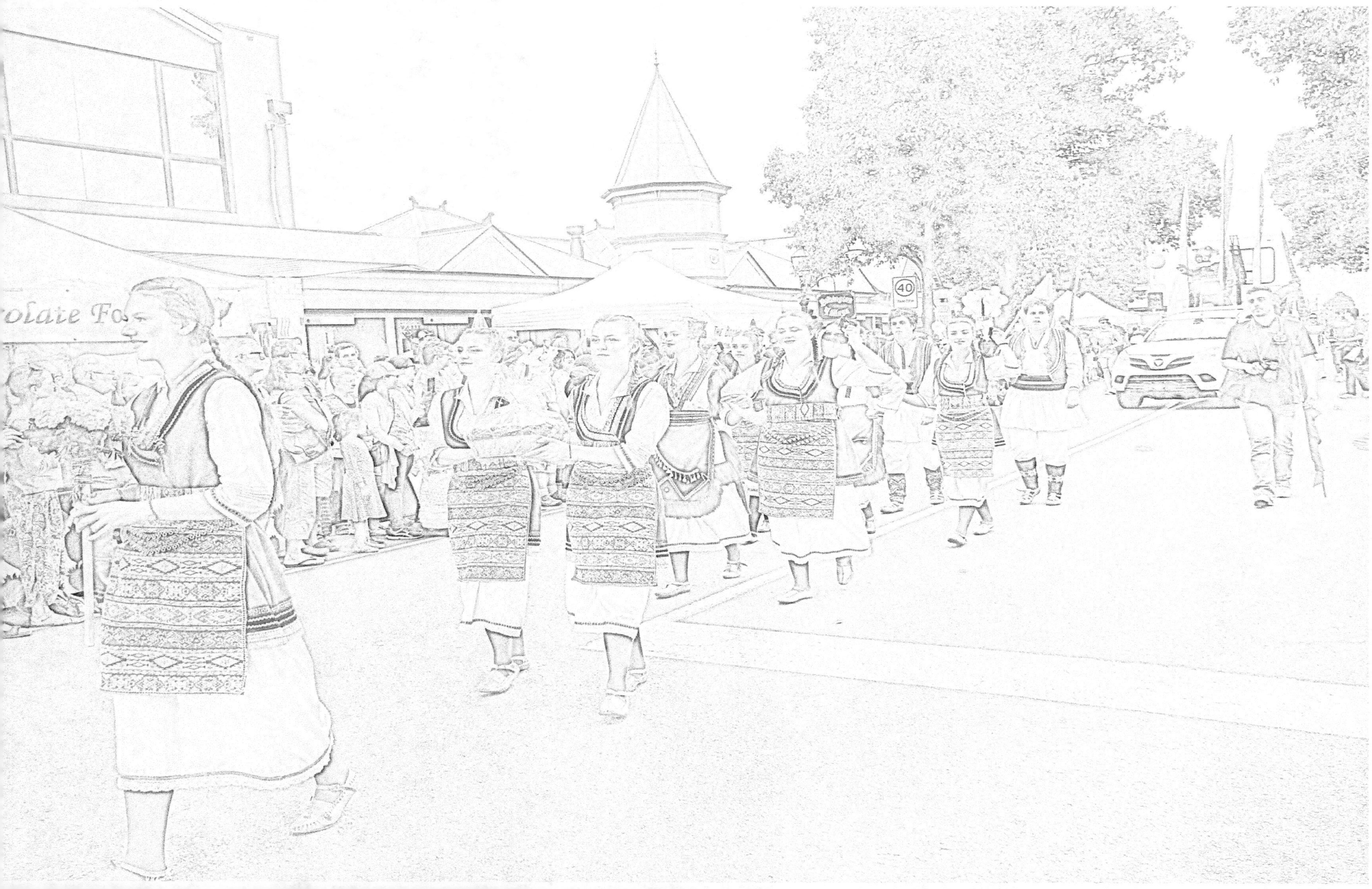
40

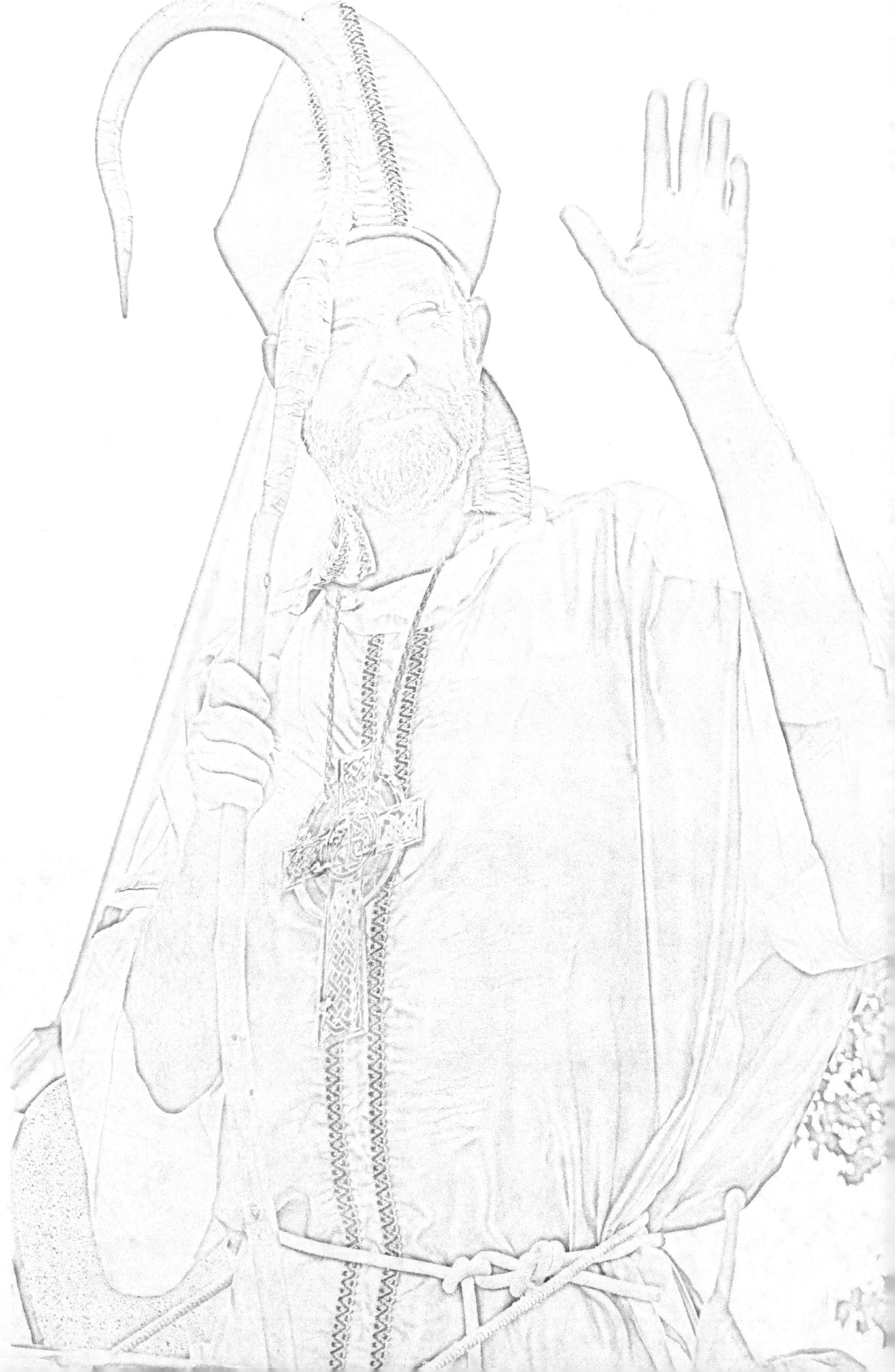

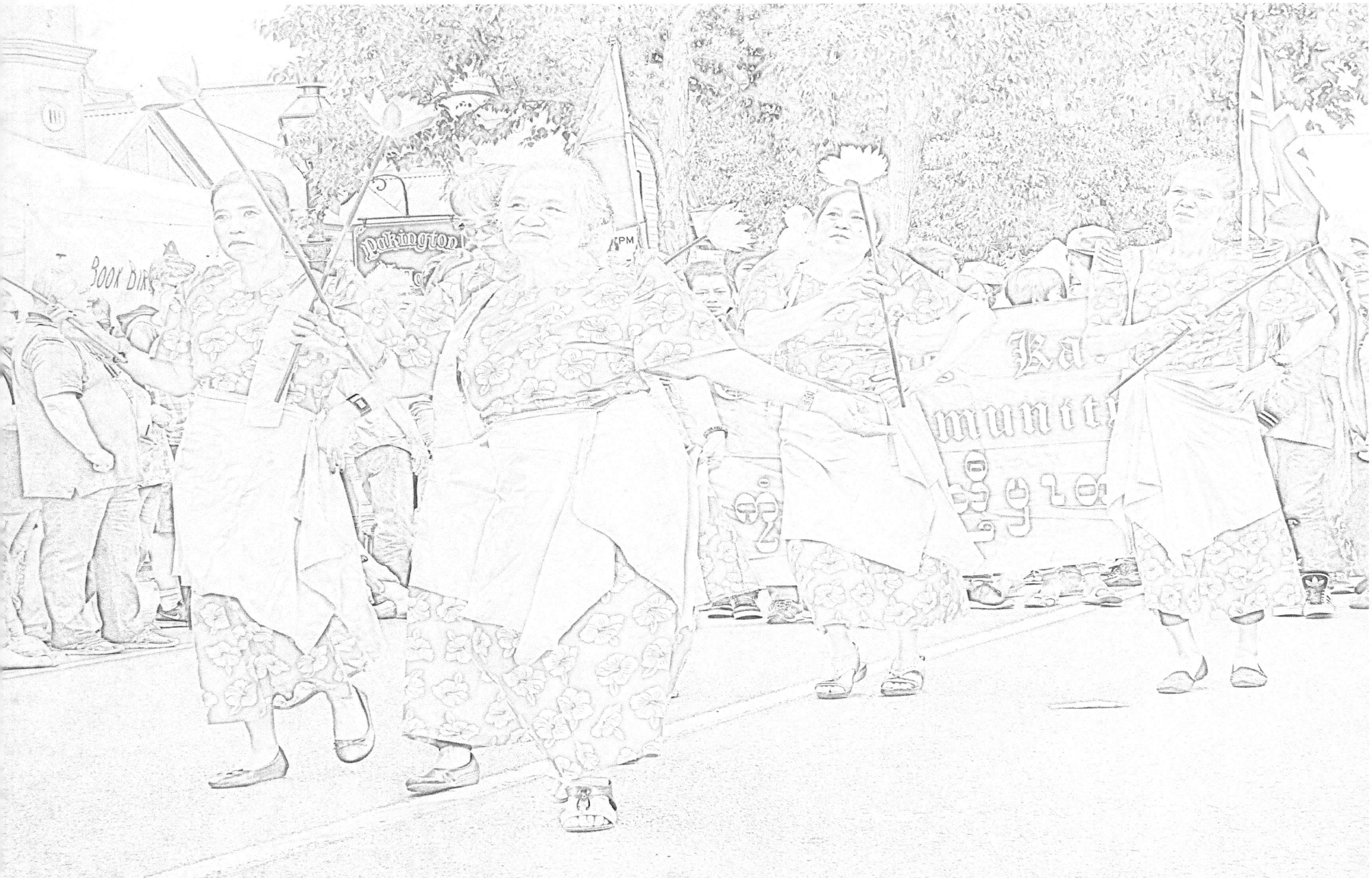
Pakington

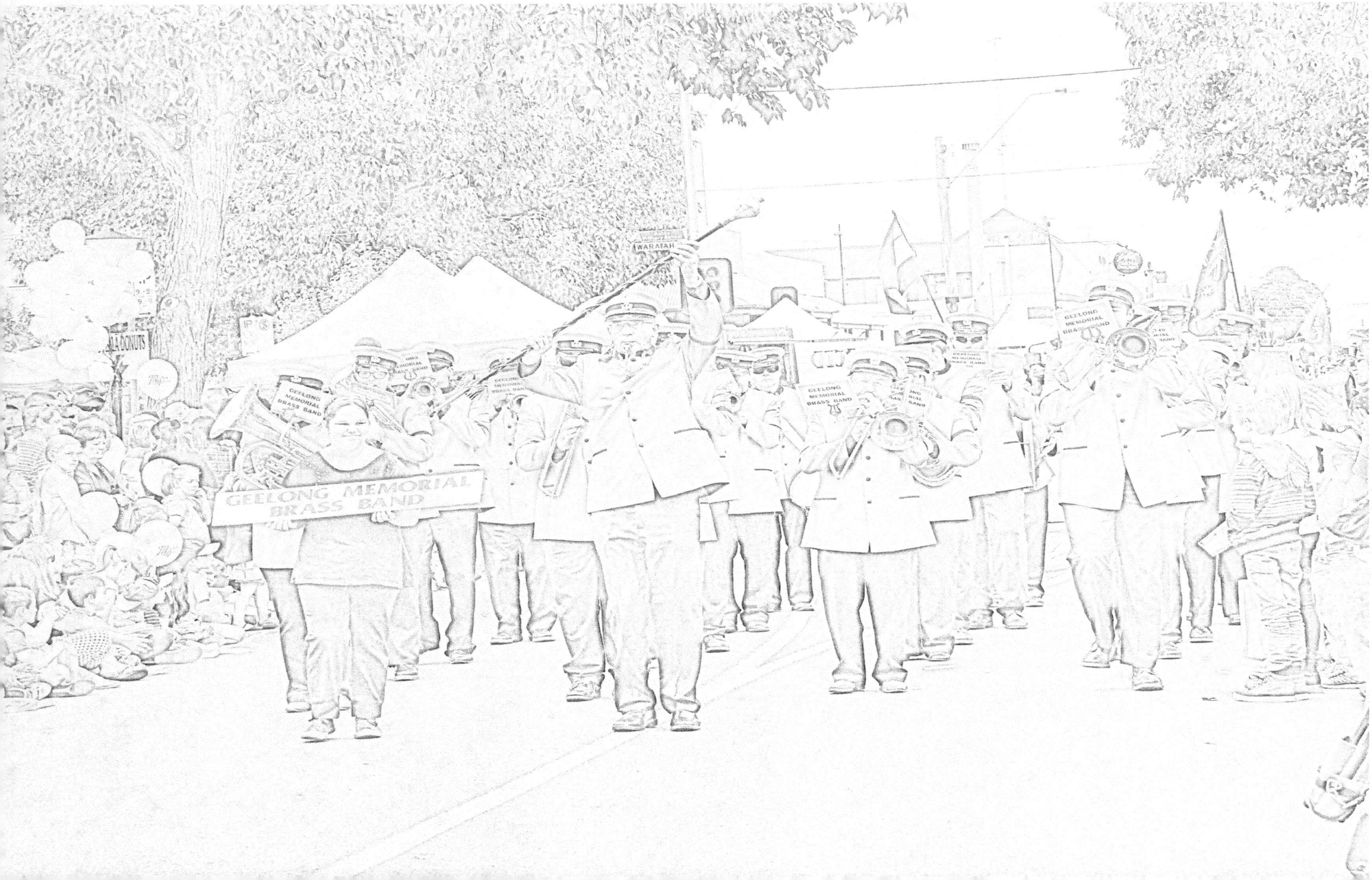
GEELONG MEMORIAL
BRASS BAND
GEELONG
MEMORIAL
BRASS BAND
WARATAH

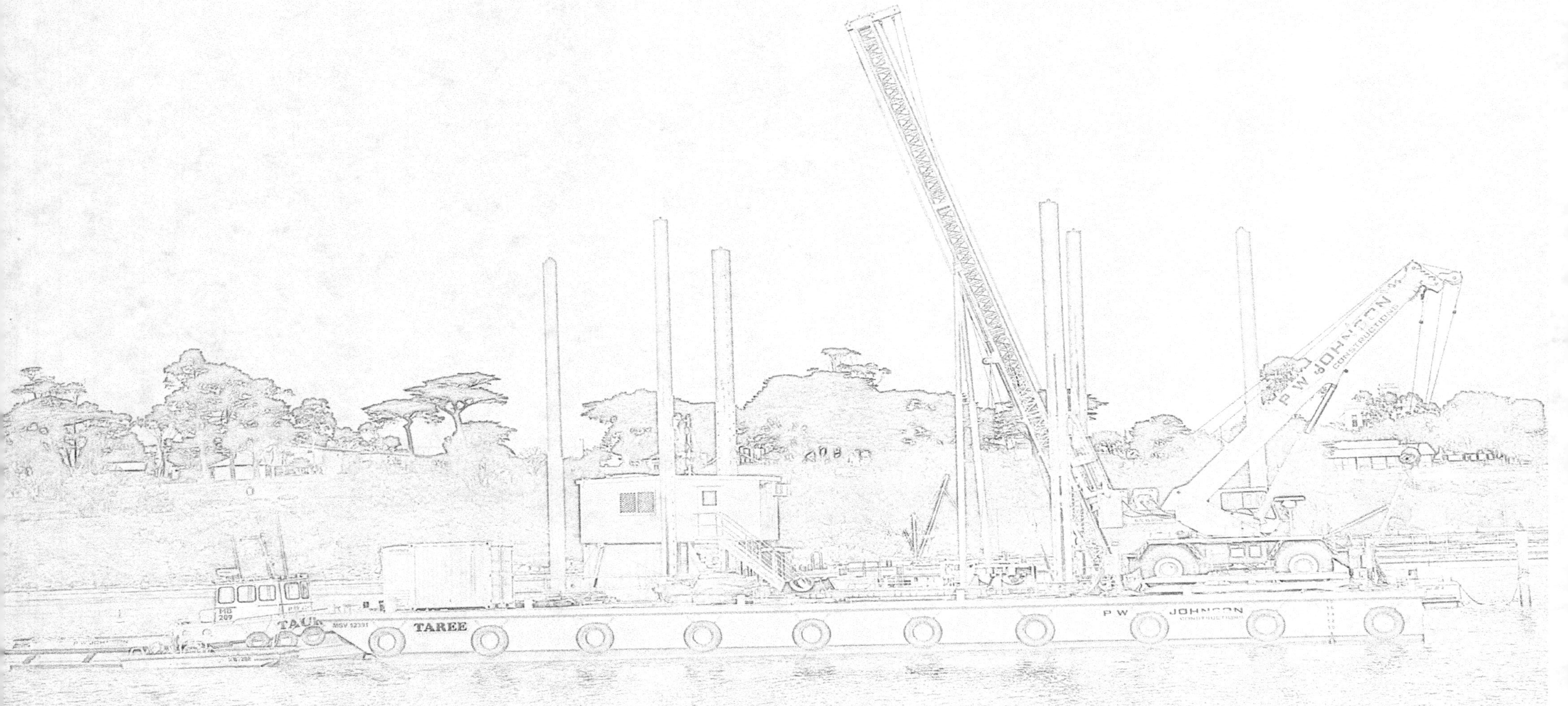
P W JOHNSON CONSTRUCTIONS
TAREE
P W JOHNSON CONSTRUCTIONS

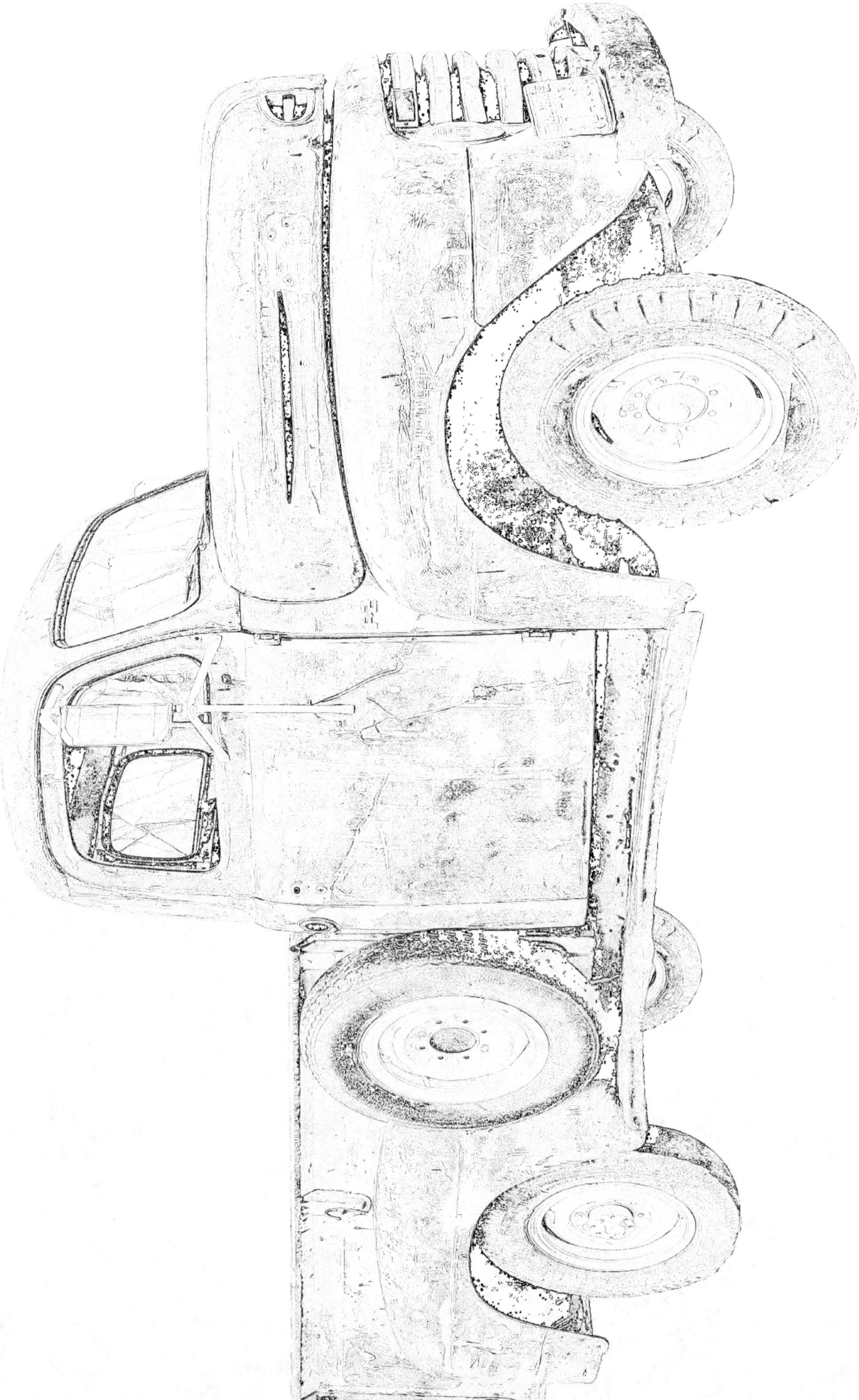

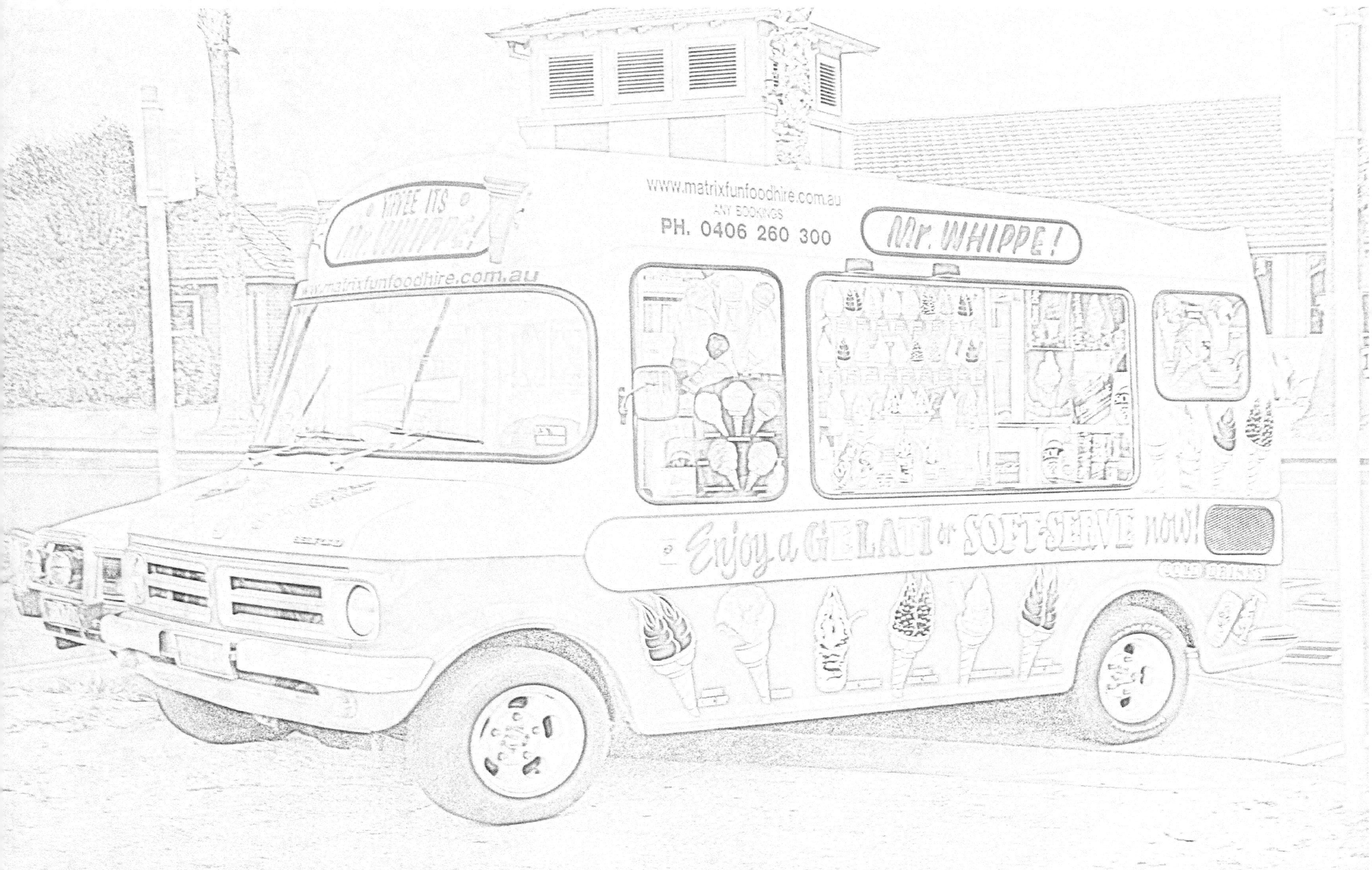
www.matrixfunfoodhire.com.au
ANY BOOKINGS
PH. 0406 260 300
Mr. WHIPPE!
Mr. WHIPPE!
www.matrixfunfoodhire.com.au
Enjoy a GELATI or SOFT-SERVE now!

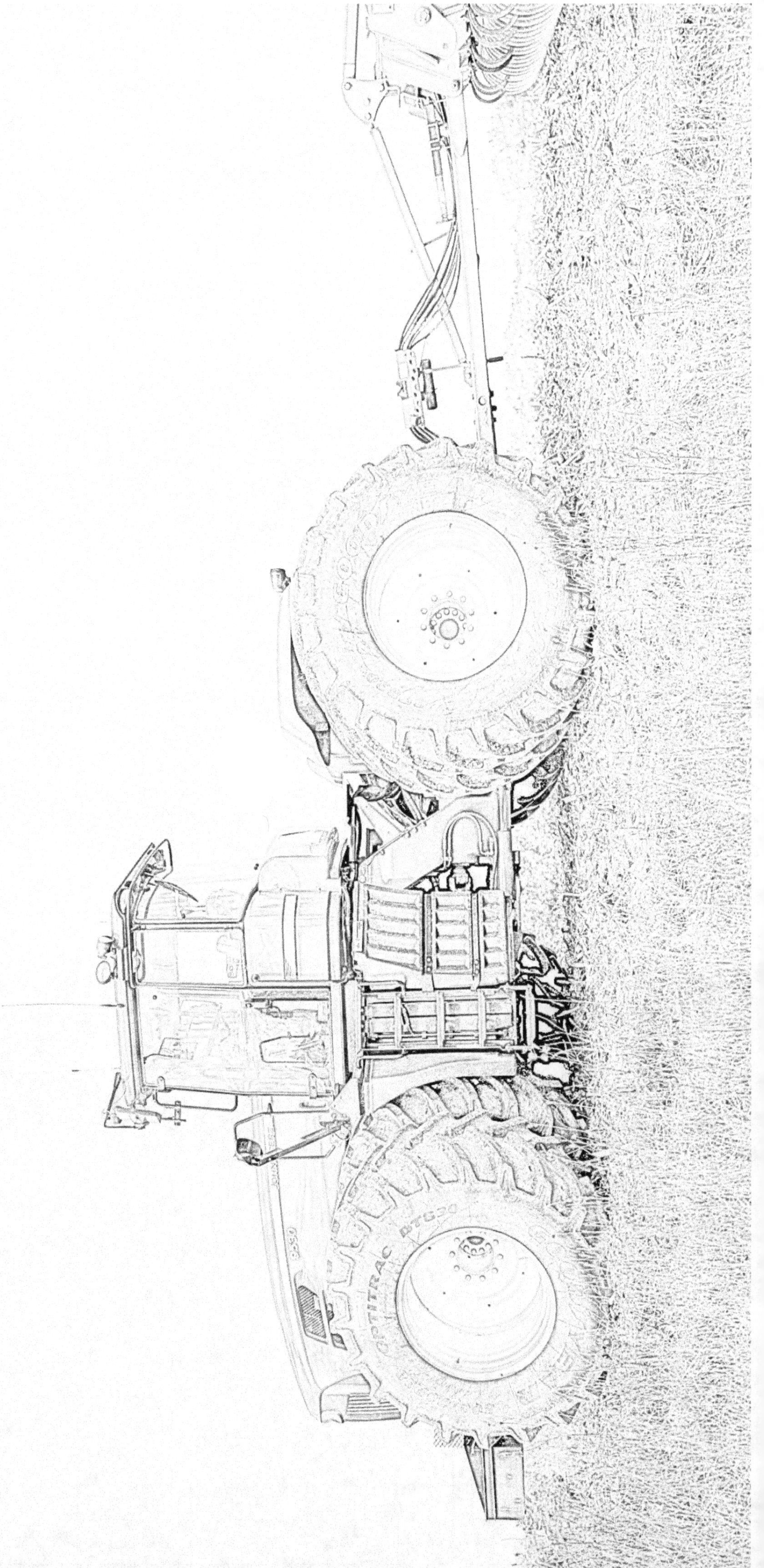

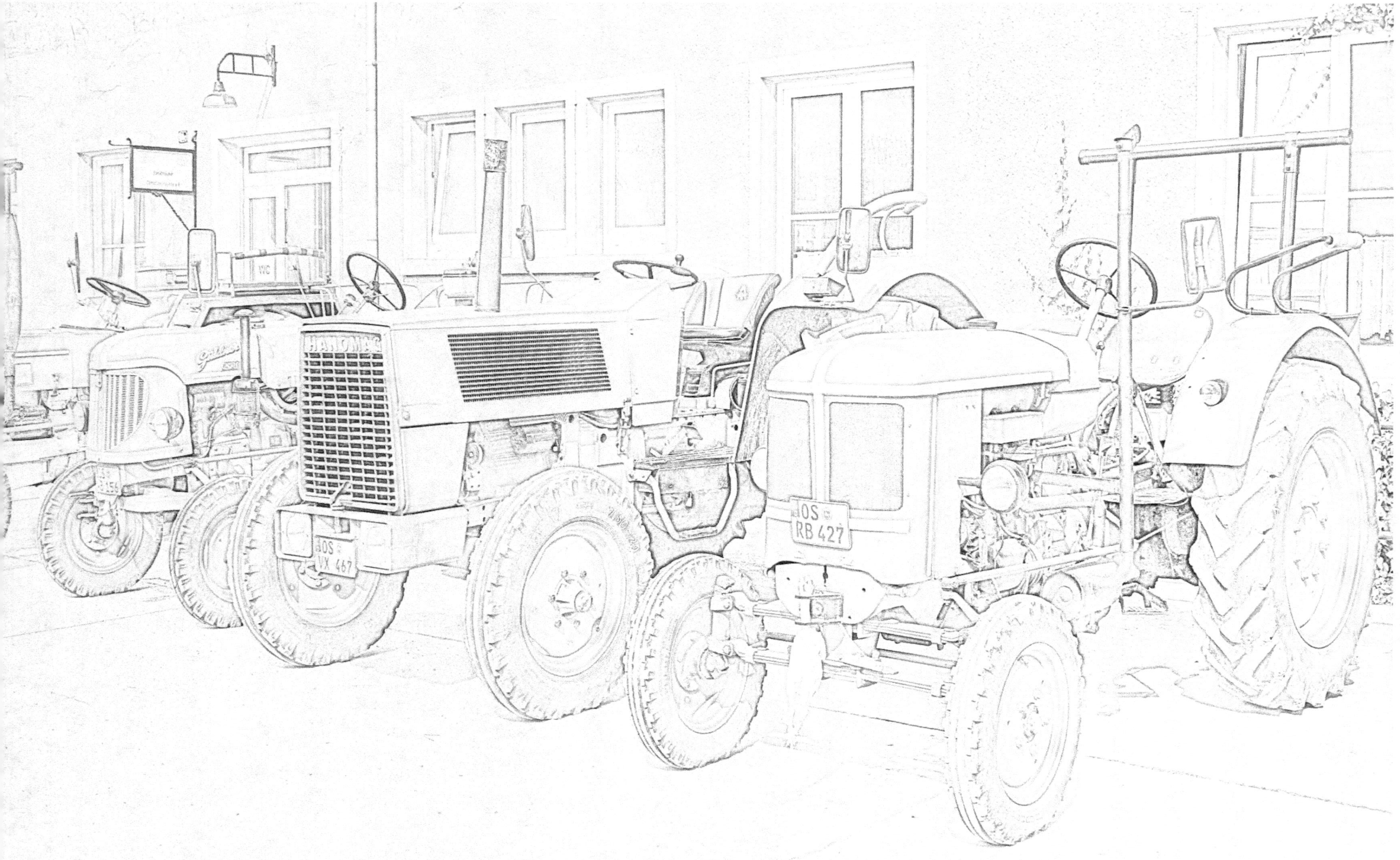

HANOMAG
OS VX 467
OS RB 427

BRIDIE O'REILLY'S
NO
ENTRY

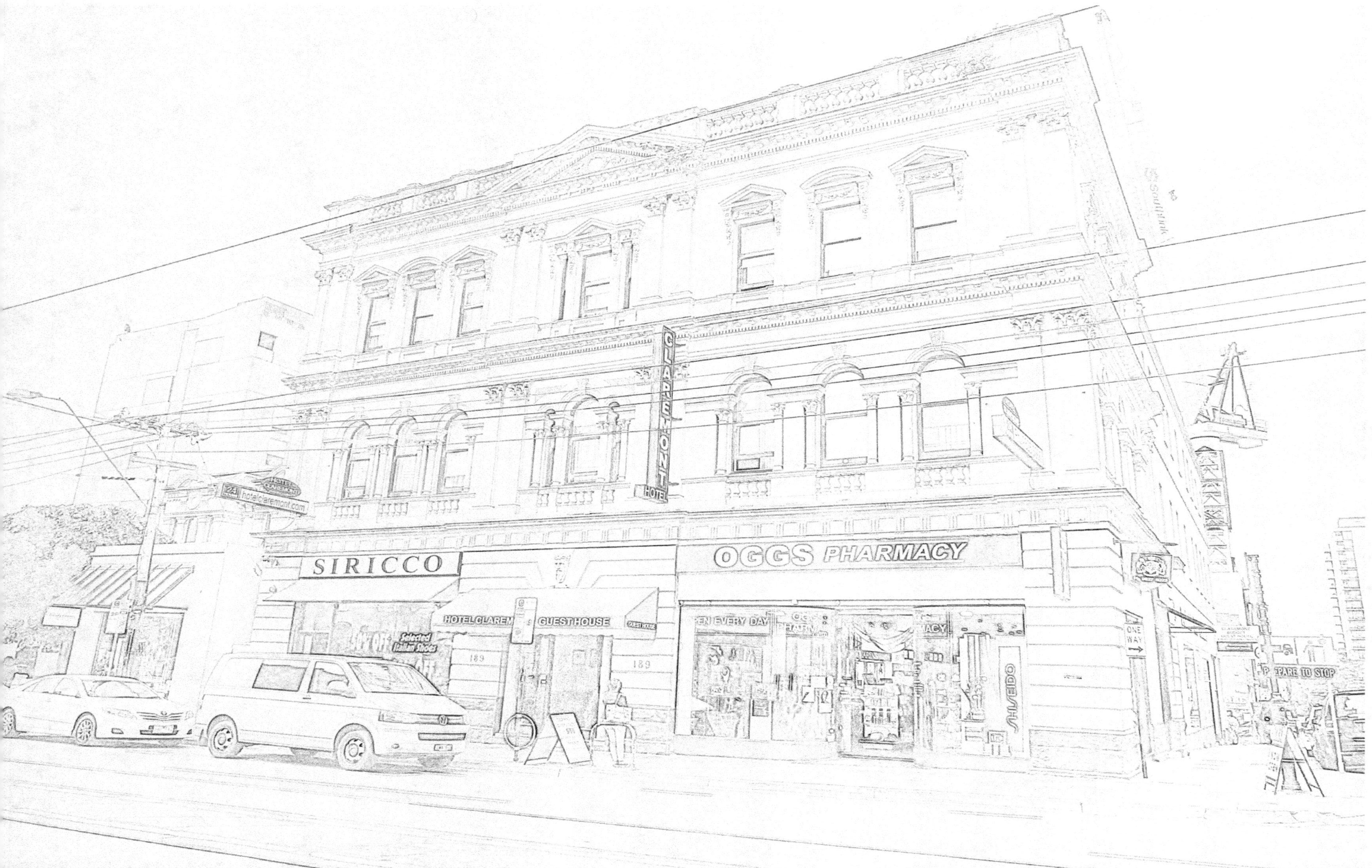
CLAREMONT
HOTEL
24 hotelclaremont.com
SIRICCO
HOTEL CLAREM
GUESTHOUSE
Selected Italian Shoes
189
189
OGGS PHARMACY
EN EVERY DAY
SHISEIDO
ONE WAY
PREPARE TO STOP

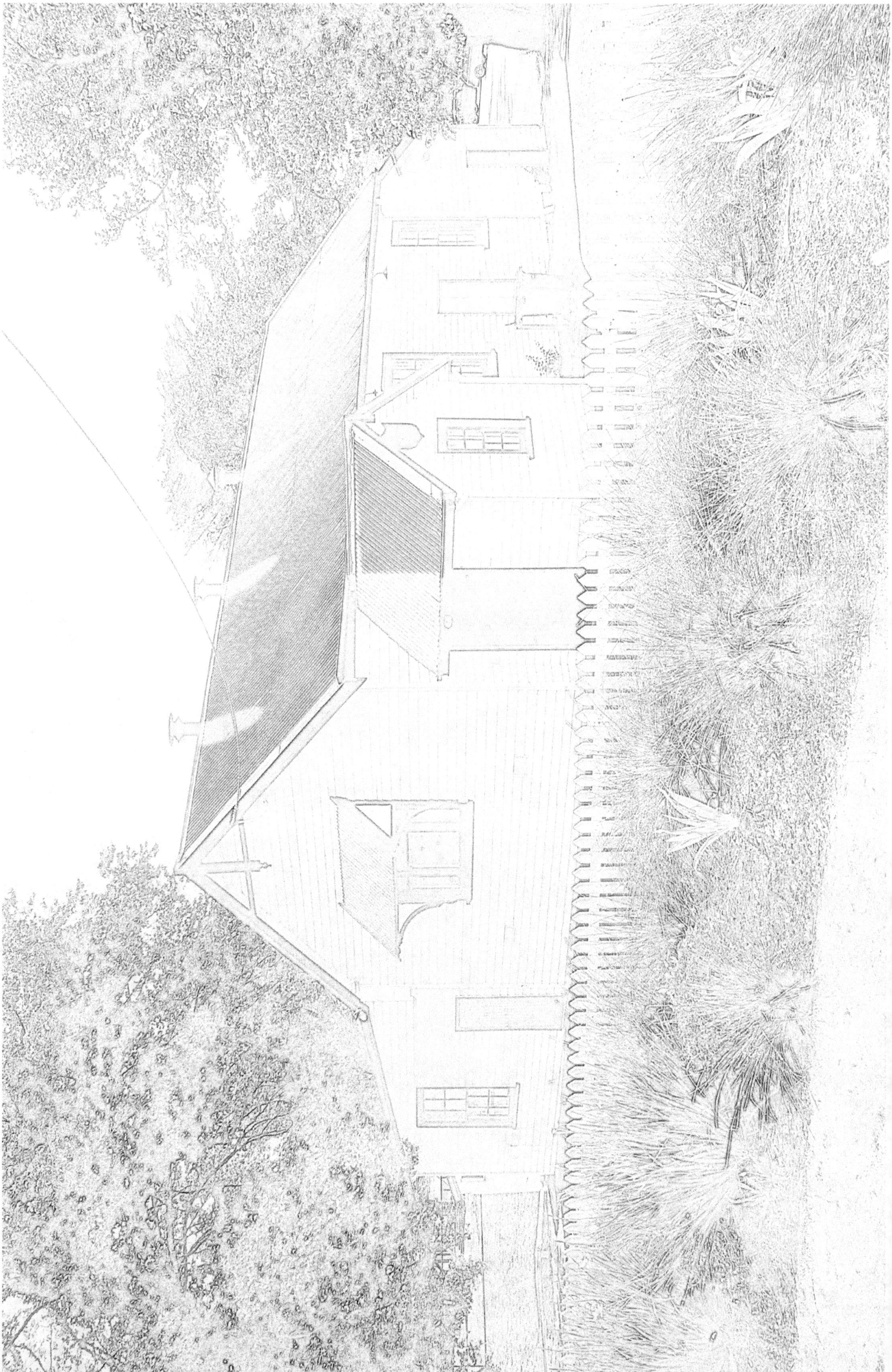

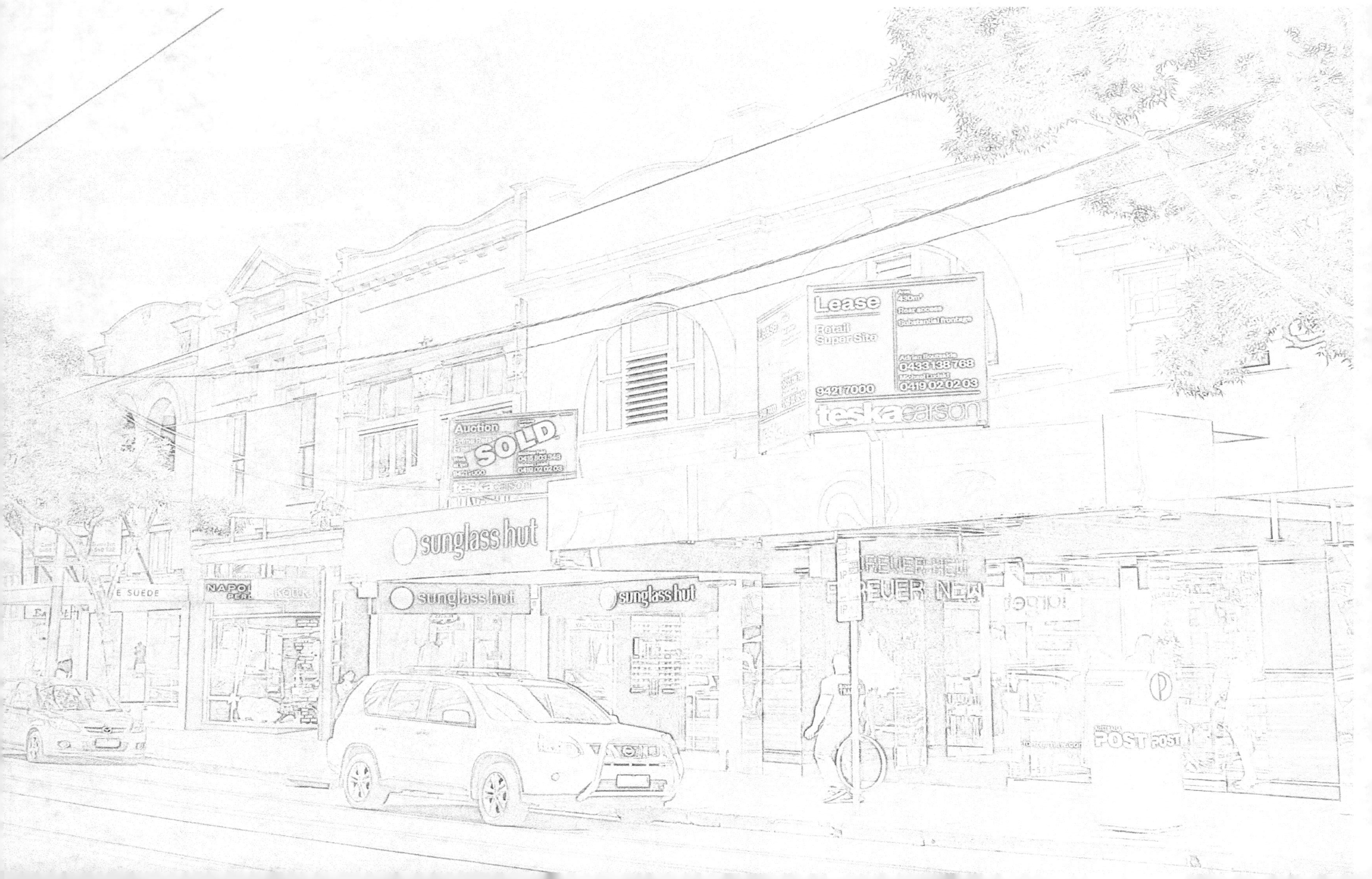
Lease
Retail
Super Site
Rear access
Substantial frontage
0433 138 768
0419 02 02 03
9421 7000
teskacarson
Auction
SOLD
teskacarson
sunglass hut
sunglass hut
sunglass hut
FOREVER NEW
POST

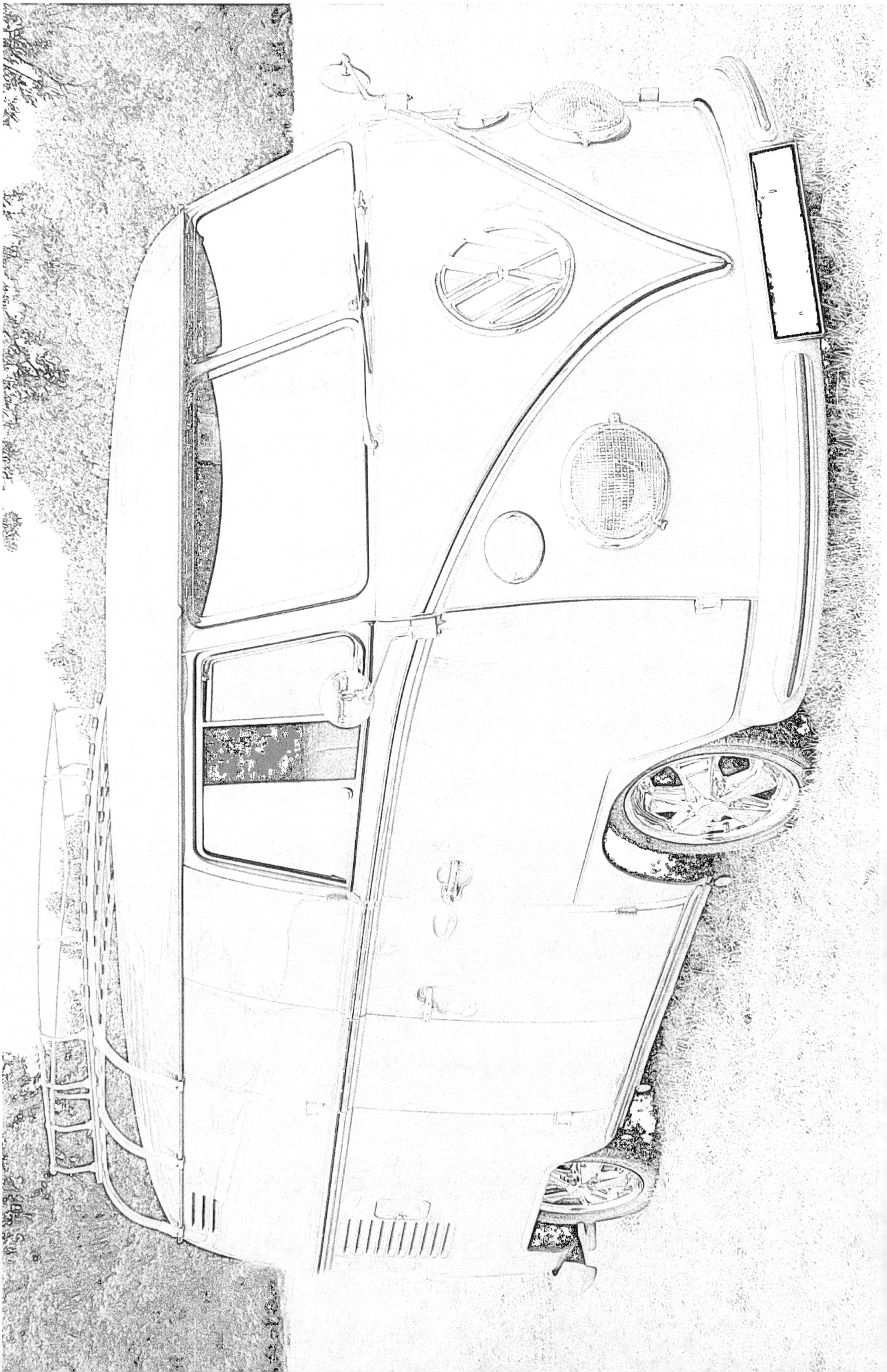

www.ingramcontent.com/pod-product-compliance
Lightning Source LLC
Chambersburg PA
CBHW080032210526
45170CB00016B/1769